The Control and Management of Communicable Disease

A Short Guide for Nurses, Doctors and Environmental Health Officers

ROY PILSWORTH, M.D.
Director, Public Health Laboratory,
Chelmsford, Essex

LONDON
H. K. LEWIS & Co. LTD
1980

First Published 1980

©

H. K. LEWIS & Co. LTD
1980

Text set in 10/12 pt. VIP Baskerville, printed and
bound in Great Britain at The Pitman Press, Bath

THE CONTROL AND MANAGEMENT
OF COMMUNICABLE DISEASE

PREFACE

It is the purpose of this little book to offer, in a semitabular form, information about the management of the more important infectious diseases.

Different infectious diseases may be considered as being important for different reasons: they may be common and well-known infections such as measles or herpes simplex infections; they may be common but not recognised as such, such as *Mycoplasma pneumoniae* infections; they may be common but caused by organisms with which most physicians have not yet come to grips, such as infections by adenoviruses or enteroviruses; they may be uncommon but serious infections such as anthrax or tetanus; finally they may be diseases practically unknown to occur in this country but of such a nature that they need to be excluded in patients returning from areas where the diseases occur with tact and diplomacy in order to prevent panic by the media or among the public—such diseases include Lassa fever and smallpox.

Knowledge about infectious diseases grows mainly through advances in microbiology and epidemiology and both these sciences have covered a lot of ground over the last 10 years or so. There are few clinicians who cannot obtain a full range of bacteriological and virological investigations. Practically all pathogenic bacteria can be cultured and all but the most exotic virus diseases investigated in routine microbiological laboratories in this country, so that it might be useful to list some of the important features of our knowledge of infectious diseases today.

In the field of diarrhoeal diseases, *Sh. sonnei* is far less active than it was earlier in the century but the diagnosis of enteritis has expanded to include the campylobacters and the rotaviruses; these two groups of organisms are the cause of more diagnosed cases of enteritis than all the other enteropathogenic organisms taken together. The older forms of food poisoning, such as salmonella and staphylococcal food poisoning, still flourish side by side with more recently discovered types such as that caused by the contamination of molluscs with small round viruses. *Clostridium welchii*, now called *Cl. perfringens*, has become an almost exclusively institutional cause of food poisoning as few housewives can today afford a joint of meat large enough to provide the anaerobic and slow-cooling environment that this organism needs for multiplication.

Great progress has been made in our knowledge of virus hepatitis since the discovery of "Australia antigen". Hepatitis type B virus infection may be routinely diagnosed and much is known about its behaviour. Serological tests for hepatitis type A virus infections will soon be available in peripheral as well as special laboratories and we shall soon have to familiarise ourselves with the several "Non-A, non-B" hepatitis viruses already discovered.

"New" diseases continue to appear, for instance, Lassa fever and Legionnaire's disease, although there is evidence that the latter infection was already around as early as 1947. Both these diseases burst dramatically on to the medical scene but both seem capable of causing mild and even subclinical infections, the former in Africa, the latter worldwide.

Some "old" diseases have become rarer (*e.g.* diphtheria and poliomyelitis) but only continued high vaccination acceptance rates will keep them rare. Smallpox appears to have been eradicated worldwide with the exception of some research laboratories. We may have to decide whether the smallpox virus should be treated as an endangered species like the whale or whether to suppress our feelings for conservation and thankfully get rid of it altogether and for good.

The earlier part of this century saw the golden age of bacterial and antitoxic vaccines; after the introduction of virus culture in tissue culture in 1946, vaccines were introduced against most of the important virus infections. We now have vaccines against measles, poliomyelitis, diphtheria, tetanus, pertussis, rubella and tuberculosis for routine use; against anthrax and rabies for those who work in areas where such infections occur; against yellow fever and cholera for travellers and against influenza and smallpox when the need arises. In the U.S.A. mumps vaccine is used routinely and vaccines against the important groups of meningococci and pneumococci are available. In the future vaccines may soon be available against the two commoner forms of viral hepatitis, cytomegalovirus, dental caries, malaria and perhaps even pregnancy although there will be grave difficulties in establishing that the latter condition is infective.

On the other hand both abuse and neglect of vaccination occur. Although a number of countries still demand smallpox vaccination certificates from visitors, there is now rarely any medical justification for this, the most dangerous of immunisations. Rubella vaccination has been with us for several years but so far no efficient machinery has been evolved to bring it to the women who need it. Exaggerated reports of the dangers of whooping cough vaccine, the choice of predominantly biased or ignorant spokesmen on the subject by the media and the payment of compensation to parents of brain-damaged children in the absence of any strong evidence that it had been caused by pertussis immunisation all conspired to reduce the acceptance rate of whooping cough vaccination resulting in a large epidemic and many needless deaths. In addition the fall in acceptance rate for whooping cough vaccination dragged down with it the rates for other vaccinations to an undesirably low level.

The specific treatment of virus infections has become an increasingly important matter because of the widespread use of steroids and immunosuppressive drugs and the improved survival of patients suffering from diseases affecting the immunity, such as Hodgkin's disease. When such patients as these develop a herpes or varicella infection the administration of drugs like cytarabine may be a life-saving procedure.

Although I have dealt with specific treatment when there seemed to be something worth saying, this book is more about the management of infectious diseases than the diagnosis and treatment of them. Indeed, I have used the heading "Clinical presentation" only to give the reader some indication of the circumstances under which he or she might consider diagnosing the infection concerned. I would not presume to tell experienced general practitioners how to diagnose "fevers".

I have tried to give some indication of the most suitable laboratory investigations for each infection, of the incidence of the infection, the need for notification, isolation, exclusion from school or disinfection, the incubation period, the period of infectivity when known, how to deal with contacts, something about the cause and behaviour of the infection, means of prevention available and finally the specific treatment where available.

I hope that this book will not only help general practitioners, district nurses, public health workers and others to deal with cases of infection but will also awake in them the curiosity to follow up and investigate, both epidemiologically and through the laboratory, the many fascinating aspects of infectious disease that are more often seen "on the district" than in the hospital.

Chelmsford 1979   R. Pilsworth

ACKNOWLEDGMENT AND DEDICATION

This book arose from an earlier booklet in the editing of which I played a part. That booklet, "A Guide to Infectious Diseases in an Emergency", arose in turn as an exercise devised by Dr Paddy Donaldson for members of a day release course on infectious diseases held at the Centre for Extension Training in Community Medicine. Discussion with the Area Medical Officer and the District Community Physicians in my own Health Area of Essex suggested that there was perhaps a need for a fuller work directed at a wider circle of readers. This is the result and I dedicate it to all my friends mentioned above but particularly my wife, so many of whose ideas are incorporated in it that she should have been named as a co-author.

R.P.

CONTENTS

USEFUL NAMES AND TELEPHONE NUMBERS

Title	*Name*	*Telephone Number*
National		
Department of Health and Social Security	Elephant and Castle London SE	01-407 5522
Communicable Disease Surveillance Centre	Colindale London NW9 5EQ	01-200 6868
Central Public Health Laboratory	Colindale London NW9 5HT	01-205 7041
24-hour Information on Overseas Vaccination Requirements	Heathrow Airport	01-897 4361
Local		
Medical Officer (Environmental Health)		
Chief Environmental Health Officer		
District Microbiologist		
Director, Public Health Laboratory		
Consultant in Infectious Diseases		
Regional Infectious Diseases Hospital		
School Medical Officer		
Specialist in Community Medicine (Child Health)		
Director of Social Services		
Divisional Veterinary Officer		
Area Medical Officer		

Clinical presentation

Cutaneous form—a papule appears on the exposed skin and becomes ulcerated and a few vesicles form around it; a black eschar forms in the centre and the lesion usually extends from 15 to 25 mm in diameter with marked surrounding oedema and erythema. Malaise and pyrexia are variable.

Respiratory and intestinal forms are rare.

Investigations

Two swabs are taken from the lesion, preferably from under the eschar; one is submitted dry and one in Stewart's bacteriological transport medium. Films will show a variable number of gram positive bacilli; culture will yield typical colonies of *B. anthracis*. Pathogenicity may be confirmed by animal inoculation.

Incidence

Only a handful of cases occur annually in England and Wales.

Notification

Inform M.O.E.H. on diagnosis.

Incubation period

2 to 5 days.

Isolation

The patient should be kept at home or in hospital with the lesion covered by an occlusive dressing for the first few days of antibiotic treatment, after which it will be free from anthrax bacilli.

Period of infectivity

Until antibiotics have been administered for about 48 hours.

Disinfection

Articles soiled by discharges should be burnt or autoclaved.

School exclusion

Until antibiotic treatment has been concluded.

Contacts

No action needed.

Cause and epidemiology

Bacillus anthracis may cause death from septicaemia in a variety of mammals. Their hair, hides and bones may become contaminated by this very resistant organism and persons involved in the importation, treatment or use of these substances may contract infection. Bone meal and hoof-and-horn meal have caused sporadic cases in amateur gardeners.

Prevention

1. Sterilisation of imported hides, hair and bone meal, *etc*.
2. Vaccination of persons continually exposed to infection. Two injections of 0·5 ml vaccine, with 6 weeks interval and 0·5 ml 6 months later. Vaccine is available from the Central Public Health Laboratory or through the local Public Health Laboratory.

Treatment

The organism is very susceptible to penicillin and a suggested dose is—benzyl penicillin, 1000 mg at once, 250 mg 6-hourly for 48 hours and then oral penicillin, 250 mg 4-hourly for 4 to 5 days.

Clinical presentation

1. A form of food poisoning; the patient develops a vague but disturbing malaise and weakness followed by evidence of cranial nerve involvement, such as paralysis of the eyelids or blurred vision; he then becomes unable to speak or swallow. Respiratory paralysis may result in asphyxia but there is no fever and the consciousness is not impaired. Death may occur as soon as twelve hours from the onset or as late as a week later.
2. Infantile botulism; after several days of constipation the child becomes severely hypotonic ("floppy infant"); weakness and cranial nerve paralyses follow. Sudden death may occur in an apparently healthy child.

Investigations

The responsible organism, *Cl. botulinum*, may be sought in the faeces and in food thought to have been responsible; its toxin may be looked for in food, faeces and serum. When death occurs the contents of the colon, serum and parts of the liver and spleen should be sent for examination.

Incidence

1. Food poisoning caused by *Cl. botulinum* toxin is very rare in Britain, only about 25 cases having been recorded, although two occurred as recently as 1978.
2. The prevalence of infantile botulism is unknown as it is rarely looked for. In the U.S.A. it seems that about 4% of sudden deaths in infants under the age of six months may be due to this disease.

Notification

When contracted as food poisoning the disease is statutorily notifiable.

Incubation period

1. Food poisoning—a few hours.
2. Infantile type—probably a few days.

Isolation

Not needed.

Period of infectivity

Not infectious.

Disinfection

Not especially indicated.

School exclusion

Until clinically well.

Contacts

Surveillance of contacts who have eaten the food suspected of causing the disease in others should be carried out for their own benefit.

Cause and epidemiology

Clostridium botulinum is a heat resistant, toxigenic anaerobe, living in the soil and in river and marine silt. Industrial canning of food is exceptionally safe, only three cases of botulism having been caused in this way in 40 years but less efficient methods of preserving food allow the organism to proliferate and produce its toxin, so that the disease is commonest where home canning is widely practised and where such dishes as fermented or rotting fish are habitually consumed. It has been observed recently that the organism may occasionally proliferate in the gut of infants under the age of 6 months, causing severe illness and sometimes unexplained sudden death.

Prevention

1. Commercially canned foods may be relied upon.
2. Home canners should be educated to use pressure cookers.
3. Local customs involving the eating of rotting fish, pickled salmon eggs, *etc.* should be discouraged.

Treatment

1. Trivalent antitoxin (100,000 units) should be given immediately.
2. The prognosis, especially in the infantile type, depends very much on good nursing with full supportive treatment in an intensive care unit.

BRUCELLOSIS

Clinical presentation

A systemic illness of acute or insidious onset with pyrexia that may sometimes be intermittent. There is usually marked weakness with sweating, rigours, arthralgia and general aching.

Investigations

Blood cultures should be taken and inoculated at the bedside; these may yield *Br. abortus* on incubation in carbon dioxide; paired sera may show a rise in agglutinating antibody in acute cases. Chronic cases may prove difficult to diagnose as farmers, veterinary surgeons, *etc.* may possess residual antibody from remote infections; complement fixation tests and the detection of specific IgM may be useful in these cases.

Incidence

About 100 cases are diagnosed each year in England and Wales.

Notification

The disease is not notifiable to the local authority but is prescribed under the Industrial Injury Scheme when the patient works in association with bovine animals or in a laboratory handling *Br. abortus*. The Chief Environmental Health Officer and the Divisional Veterinary Officer should be notified.

Incubation period

More than 10 days, up to 2 years.

Isolation

Not needed.

Period of infectivity

Patients are not infectious.

Disinfection

Not especially indicated.

School exclusion

Until clinically well.

Contacts

No action needed.

Cause and epidemiology

Brucella abortus causes infectious abortion of cows (a similar effect in humans is almost unknown). Farmers and veterinary surgeons may become infected from products of conception. Sporadic cases may be caused by drinking unpasteurised milk and laboratory infections have occurred.

Brucella melitensis, the cause of Malta fever, may rarely cause brucellosis in this country.

Prevention

Complete eradication of *Br. abortus* from herds in this country as has been done elsewhere.

Pasteurisation of milk supplies.

Hygienic disposal of products of conception from aborted cows.

Treatment

Acute cases are usually amenable to treatment but chronic cases may be little improved by antibiotics. Tetracycline (2 to 3 g/day for 21 days) is the drug of choice but streptomycin (1 g daily) may be given with it.

CYTOMEGALOVIRUS INFECTION *Not notifiable*

Clinical presentation
1. Congenital infection; microcephaly, cerebral calcification, jaundice, failure to thrive, mental retardation.
2. Acquired infection:
   a. "Glandular fever with a negative Paul-Bunnell";
   b. Pyrexia after blood transfusion–usually mild;
   c. Infection in immunosuppressed patients or with leukaemia or Hodgkin's disease, *etc.*—often severe.

Investigations
Fresh urine may show epithelial cells with typical inclusions. Swabs may be taken by rubbing them firmly against the inside of the baby's cheeks and submitted in virus transport medium; these may yield the virus when cultured on human fibroblasts. Paired sera show a rise in complement fixing antibody.

Notification
None needed.

Incubation period
Not known.

Isolation
Not needed.

Period of infectivity
Babies and immunodeficient patients remain infectious for long periods. "Reactivation" of the dormant virus occurs during pregnancy occasionally and the virus is excreted in the milk and from the cervix.

Disinfection
Not especially indicated.

School exclusion
Until clinically well.

Contacts
No action needed.

Incidence

In England and Wales 40 to 50% of women of childbearing age have been previously affected and thus are immune. These will not become infected in pregnancy although they may "reactivate"; their specific antibody will pass across the placenta and protect the baby. The remainder of pregnant women (50 to 60%) are still susceptible and a small percentage develop the infection during pregnancy. In less developed countries all women will have been infected early in life so that the congenital form of the infection is unknown there.

Cause and epidemiology

Infection is always acquired from a human excretor. Animal cytomegaloviruses are species specific and so do not infect man. The main importance of the disease is the severity of many congenital infections. About 1% of babies are born with the infection and 90% of these have no symptoms. Of the latter 10 to 20% and of those *with* symptoms about 50% will not develop normally when compared with uninfected control babies.

Prevention

A vaccine has been prepared and used in volunteers but the ethical difficulties besetting the use of human herpes-type virus vaccines make it unlikely that such a vaccine will be generally introduced in the near future.

Clinical presentation

The onset of the illness is usually insidious with headache, rigours and a pyrexia gradually increasing over a few days to about 40°C. The patient often appears extremely ill, the spleen may be enlarged and a sparse rash ("rose spots") may be present over the abdomen, chest or back.

Investigations

Blood culture should yield the causative organism during the first 7 to 10 days; at least three cultures should be taken. Faeces may yield the causative organism from the first week onward, more frequently as time progresses. Several stool specimens should be taken as excretion may be intermittent.

The urine may yield the organism, but irregularly (about 30% of cases) in the first week or so.

Agglutination tests are useful if they show a high level of antibodies to an organism that could cause enteric fever and low levels to all others; previous infection or TAB vaccination may confuse the picture as, in these cases, antibodies to enteric organisms may be non-specifically stimulated in some non-enteric infections, such as glandular fever. If two specimens of serum, taken with an interval of ten days, show a fourfold or greater rise in titre to one single enteric organism, this is diagnostic.

Incidence

In England and Wales there are, each year, about 250 cases of typhoid fever, 40 of paratyphoid A and 80 of paratyphoid B.

Notification

Statutory, to the M.O.E.H. If there are reasonable grounds for suspicion, notify him informally before laboratory confirmation has been obtained.

Incubation period

2 to 42 days, but usually 3 weeks or less.

Isolation

The patient should remain in an infectious disease hospital or an isolation block until clinically fit. Excretion of salmonella organisms should not hinder discharge as long as the patient is cooperative and responsible.

Period of infectivity

S. typhi may be excreted for a variable time after recovery; after a year the person is described as a chronic carrier as opposed to a convalescent excreter. About 3% of cases are still excreting after a year.

Disinfection

Soiled articles should be disinfected; in countries where sewage disposal methods are deficient faeces and urine should also be disinfected, but in civilised countries excreta may usually be disposed of down the sewer.

School exclusion

This is at the discretion of the M.O.E.H. and will depend on the age of the child and whether or not the organism is still being excreted.

Contacts

1. For the purpose of tracing the source of the infection.
   If a specific meal or catering establishment is concerned then faeces and urine of all connected with it should be examined bacteriologically.
2. For the purpose of detecting secondary cases or cases infected at the same time as the index case.
   All such contacts should be under surveillance for 3 weeks and after this time three consecutive stool specimens should be examined; if these are negative and there has been no febrile illness during the period, then surveillance may be lifted. Contacts who are food handlers or who deal with small children should be excluded from work until the end of the surveillance period.

Cause and epidemiology

Infection is always from a human case or carrier, usually *via* food or water. *S. typhi* can cause infection in a very small dosage so that, even when the contaminating unit is greatly diluted, as in a water supply, infection may still occur. The paratyphoid organisms can only cause infection when present in large numbers, so that food, in which they can proliferate, rather than water, is the common infecting material. The organisms multiply in cells of the reticuloendothelial system during the incubation period and from there they pass into the bloodstream at the beginning of the illness proper. They then infect the target organs, usually lymphoid patches in the wall of the large intestine. Abscesses that form here may ulcerate, causing bowel perforation or haemorrhage, usually during the third week of the illness.

Prevention

1. Control of carriers.

   It has been estimated (1964) that there are 500 to 1000 typhoid carriers in Britain. Increased immigration over recent years may render that figure an underestimate. Persons who have suffered from typhoid fever should never again work as food handlers, either as a job or, if possible, even at home. Patients must be followed up for many years to make sure that they have not become chronic carriers and the M.O.E.H. should be consulted for details of such follow-up schemes.

   The practice of carrying out investigations on prospective waterworks employees to ensure that they are not typhoid carriers appears to be a waste of time.

2. Vaccination.

   Holidaymakers to less hygienic parts of the world, workers in microbiology laboratories and staff of infectious diseases hospitals should be vaccinated against typhoid fever. The A and B constituents of TAB have little protective value and cause febrile reactions, so that it is best to give two intradermal injections of monovalent typhoid vaccine into the skin over the deltoid area with a 2 to 4 week interval.

Treatment

Antibiotics such as chloramphenicol and ampicillin and drugs such as cotrimoxazole have reduced the mortality of typhoid fever and cut down the period of severe pyrexia.

Note

Enteric fever includes typhoid fever, paratyphoid A, paratyphoid B and paratyphoid C as well as enteric-like illnesses due to other salmonella species which, although usually causing food poisoning, sometimes cause a septicaemia. Although typhoid fever is referred to in the text, the latter applies equally to other enteric fevers except that they are not usually as severe as typhoid fever and less stringent attitudes need be taken in the matter of following up patients.

The viruses of this group are each capable of causing a number of different forms of illness indistinguishable from those caused by some other agents, ranging from pharyngitis to lymphocytic meningitis. They may also cause fairly specific syndromes such as poliomyelitis or Bornholm disease.

The *picornaviruses* are small (20 to 30 nm) spherical viruses that contain RNA. The group is subdivided as follows:

Human Picornaviruses

1. Enteroviruses   Types
   a. Poliovirus   1 to 3
   b. Coxsackie A   1 to 22, 24
   c. Coxsackie B   1 to 6
   d. Echoviruses   1 to 9, 11 to 27, 29 to 33
   e. Enteroviruses   68 to 70

2. Rhinoviruses (common cold viruses)

The enteroviruses are primarily inhabitants of the cells of the gut. Occasionally they invade the bloodstream, infecting target cells such as the anterior horn cells of the cord as in poliomyelitis or the muscles in Bornholm disease. During an outbreak all forms of illness are seen and each year seems to bring forth a different epidemic type, *e.g.*, echovirus type 11 in 1978, coxsackievirus B5 in 1960.

POLIOMYELITIS *Notifiable*

Clinical presentation

An acute virus infection that occasionally causes motor neurone paralysis. The onset may be sudden with pyrexia and paralysis appearing at the same time or the disease may be preceded by a prodromal pyrexia and then a few days of normal temperature. Diarrhoea may occur during the early stages of illness and non-paralytic cases may be clinically indistinguishable from mild cases of meningitis. Occasionally there are symptoms and signs of encephalitis.

Investigations

Three consecutive daily stool specimens should be submitted in clean containers; these should yield the virus in tissue culture. Examination of the CSF will show a slight increase of cells but no organisms and the virus is rarely isolated from this site. Serological tests are of little use in diagnosis.

Incidence

There are about 20 cases each year in Britain although in more undeveloped areas, *e.g.* Brazil, there are still about 2000 cases *per annum*.

Notification

This is statutory, to the M.O.E.H., but he should be notified informally on suspicion.

Incubation period

7 to 10 days.

Isolation

Patients are usually nursed in an infectious diseases hospital, if only for expertise in nursing and the availability of respirators. It may be wise not to discharge the patient until laboratory tests indicate that excretion has ceased.

Period of infectivity

Most patients cease to excrete the virus within six weeks.

Disinfection
Not especially indicated.

School exclusion
Until clinically well.

Contacts
It is diplomatic to exclude from school children who are family contacts until shown to be free from infection by laboratory tests. All contacts should be immunised once the case has been *clinically* confirmed.

Cause and epidemiology
The poliovirus, of which there are three serological types, is acquired from a human case or carrier. The situation has changed radically in the last decade or so, as, during poliomyelitis epidemics, there was about one clinical case for each hundred or so infections. Today carriers seem almost as rare as cases and the former are usually infected by vaccine strains following immunisation of themselves or their fellows. In poorer countries the virus may be widespread, affecting most children before their second birthday. There is a high infantile mortality but little diagnosable poliomyelitis; when a susceptible person arrives, as did British soldiers during the last war, the risk of contracting a severe attack of the disease is great.

Prevention
Vaccination has reduced the number of cases in the U.S.A. from about 40,000 cases *per annum* in 1951 to 20 in 1977. In Britain the figures have fallen from about 4000 to about 20 over the same period.

Cases that do occur do so usually in children who have not been immunised and in Holland in 1978 a fairly large number of cases occurred in members of a religious sect with objections to immunisation. To keep the prevalence of poliomyelitis at its present low level in this country it is essential to maintain a high acceptance rate of the vaccine.

The vaccine in use in Britain is a live attenuated mixture of the three types. Three doses are given during the first year of life, one at school entry and one is recommended on leaving school.

Travellers overseas should receive a further dose if it seems advisable.

There is a very slight risk of the vaccine strain causing the infection. About one case of poliomyelitis in about 12 million immunising doses cannot be ruled out as having not been caused by the vaccine. On these grounds the D.H.S.S. has suggested that where a child's parents have not been previously vaccinated they should be done at the same time as the child (see p. 128).

When outbreaks occur the M.O.E.H. may be expected to set up vaccination centres once the infection has been confirmed virologically and the type of virus determined.

Treatment

There is no specific treatment; once the acute phase of the illness is over residual paralysis should be treated by the physiotherapist and the orthopaedic surgeon.

COXSACKIEVIRUS A INFECTION *Notifiable only as acute meningitis*

Clinical presentation

1. Lymphocytic meningitis.

   The onset is usually sudden with the classic signs of meningitis although there may be only a severe headache. The patient is not usually as ill as with pyogenic meningitis and the CSF is clear or only slightly turbid. Illness may be preceded by diarrhoea or a minor illness about a week previously. Recovery usually occurs rapidly.

2. Paralysis.

   In a few cases the symptoms of meningitis are followed by a poliomyelitis-like paralysis; this usually clears up but very rarely is permanent.

3. Herpangina.

   This consists of the acute onset of small discrete vesicles over the rear of the buccal cavity, on the palate, the fauces and the pharynx. These vesicles rupture to produce ulcers about 5 mm in diameter and they are usually accompanied with pyrexia and headache. They are very painful, there is often secondary infection and the regional lymph nodes are enlarged. The condition resembles in many ways a primary herpes simplex infection.

4. Acute pharyngitis.

   This resembles herpangina but no ulceration occurs.

5. Hand, foot and mouth disease.

   This is a mild infection in children with small vesicles in the mouth, the palms and soles and often on the skin surrounding the anus. This infection often occurs in small outbreaks in children of a housing estate and probably is another manifestation of primary infection. Most cases are due to types 10, 16 and 5, in order of prevalence. The disease is not, of course, related to foot and mouth disease of cattle.

6. Acute haemorrhagic conjunctivitis.

   Although described mainly in Africa this disease is caused by type 24 and enterovirus type 70, so that it is worthwhile to look for these viruses in cases of haemorrhagic conjunctivitis occurring in Britain.

7. Non-specific infections.

   The majority of coxsackievirus A infections are probably either completely subclinical or nonspecific infections with malaise, fever and possibly a rash which may be erythematous or maculopapular.

Investigations

The virus may be isolated from throat swabs or faeces but, as it can be isolated only by animal inoculation, few laboratories can undertake the procedure; however, when the diagnosis is important arrangements can usually be made. Serological diagnosis is not practicable.

Incidence

It is likely that these viruses behave like the other enteroviruses so that, each year, many undiagnosed infections occur. It is also likely that a different epidemic strain becomes prevalent most years, but the difficulty in isolating these viruses make this difficult to prove.

Notification

Only when the infection occurs in the form of acute meningitis.

Incubation period

Not known, probably 7 to 10 days.

Isolation

Not needed.

Period of infectivity

Not known for certain but probably up to about 4 weeks.

Disinfection

Not especially indicated.

School exclusion

Until clinically well.

Contacts

No action needed.

Cause and epidemiology

The 23 types of coxsackievirus A are typical enteroviruses although few grow well in tissue culture and isolation is by the inoculation of suckling mice, in which widespread myositis and flaccid paralysis occur. The virus multiplies in the human gut and between outbreaks it is kept going by carriers and sporadic cases.

Prevention

There is no practical method but if a particular type should prove a serious problem there is little doubt that a vaccine could be made as in the case of poliomyelitis.

Treatment

There is no specific treatment; antibiotics are not indicated.

COXSACKIEVIRUS B INFECTION *Notifiable only as acute meningitis*

Clinical presentation
1. Lymphocytic meningitis. (See Coxsackievirus A infection, p. 16)
2. Paralysis.
3. Pyrexia with a rash.
4. Acute upper respiratory tract infection.
5. Pleurodynia, myalgia, Bornholm disease.
6. Myocarditis of the newborn.
7. Myocarditis and pericarditis of adults.
8. Undifferentiated febrile illness.

Investigations
Coxsackieviruses B are usually easily grown in tissue culture. Throat swabs (in virus transport medium), faeces and CSF may be submitted.

Incidence
Very common. Sporadic cases of various types of virus occur throughout the year and in epidemic years large outbreaks of a particular type occur. Recognised cases represent only a small proportion of the total number of infections.

Notification
Only when the infection takes the form of acute meningitis.

Incubation period
Not known for certain, probably 7 to 10 days.

Isolation
Not needed.

Period of infectivity
Not known for certain—probably up to about 4 weeks.

Disinfection
Not especially indicated.

School exclusion
Until clinically well.

Contacts

No action is needed but in the interests of epidemiology, stools may be submitted for examination, especially from institutional outbreaks.

Cause and epidemiology

There are 6 serologically distinct types of coxsackievirus B. All will grow in tissue culture and cause spastic paralysis in suckling mice. They multiply in the epithelial cells of the human gut and occasionally cause disease which may be nonspecific, such as meningitis, or typical, such as Bornholm disease.

Prevention

No practicable method is available.

Treatment

There is no specific treatment. Antibiotics are not indicated.

ECHOVIRUS INFECTION
Notifiable only as acute meningitis

Clinical presentation

1. Lymphocytic meningitis. (See Coxsackievirus A infection, p. 16)
2. Paralysis.
3. Rash with pyrexia.
4. Acute upper respiratory tract infection.
5. Enteritis.
6. Death with renal involvement in young infants.
7. Undifferentiated febrile disease.

Investigations

Throat swabs (in virus transport medium), stools and CSF may be inoculated into fibroblasts or primary monkey kidney cells. The presence of virus in the stools only does not necessarily indicate that it is the cause of the symptoms.

Incidence

Very common, especially in epidemic periods, when the number of recognised infections is a very small proportion of the total number of infections.

Notification

Only when the disease takes the form of acute meningitis.

Incubation period

Probably 7 to 10 days.

Isolation

Not usually needed, but infected babies should be kept away from other young babies.

Period of infectivity

Probably up to about 4 weeks.

Disinfection

Not especially indicated.

School exclusion

Until clinically well.

Contacts

No action needed except for epidemiological considerations.

Cause and epidemiology

Although the 31 types of echovirus normally multiply in the human gut they do seem to be spread by droplets more often than other enteroviruses. Most infections are symptomless and outbreaks due to specific types occur. A disturbing factor is the emerging ability of some types (type 11, for instance) to cause fatal illness in young babies and probably also occasional "cot deaths".

Prevention

No practicable method is available.

Treatment

No specific treatment is available; antibiotics are not indicated.

Smallpox
Lassa fever
Virus haemorrhagic fevers—
     Marburg disease (green monkey disease)
     Ebola fever

These diseases are unlikely to occur in Britain but each year there are a number of suspected cases and it is important to have a plan of action available to deal with patients recently returned from abroad or working in establishments harbouring these viruses in whom one of these infections may be suspected.

It is important that these diseases are not lightly diagnosed because, as soon as the suspicion is committed to paper, it is the duty of the M.O.E.H. to put into operation measures designed to reduce the risk of secondary cases arising and these methods are expensive in terms of both money and manpower. It is best to approach the matter informally, seeking the advice of the M.O.E.H. and others before arriving at any decision.

Never send the patient to the local laboratory or anywhere else once you have suspected one of these infections.

Dealing with Suspected Cases

Disease suspected	Location of patient	Patient's transport	Action
Smallpox	His home		Keep him there
Smallpox	Surgery		Keep him there
Other exotica	His home		Keep him there
	Surgery	His car	Send him home
		Public transport	Keep him at the surgery

Smallpox appears to have been eradicated except from a few virus laboratories. Lassa fever cases will have contracted the disease in West Africa. A case of Marburg disease followed accidental self inoculation in a research institute in this country. No cases of Ebola fever have yet occurred in Britain.

SMALLPOX   *Notifiable*

Clinical presentation

The patient may recently have returned from an endemic area or may be associated with an establishment where the virus is handled. He has a pyrexia with a vesicular rash; the vesicles are large, circular, thick-walled and "under" rather than "in" the skin and all about the same size; the distribution is centrifugal, the limbs being more affected than the trunk. There is no "cropping" as in chickenpox.

Having said this, the disease in vaccinated subjects is frequently modified and the patient appears less ill but remains just as infectious as a typical case.

Investigations

The local virologist and the M.O.E.H. should be consulted before any specimens are taken.

Few possible cases in this country are *seriously* suspected of being smallpox and in most cases the virologist will take specimens of vesicle fluid and examine them with the electron microscope. If the case is one of chickenpox, herpes-like virus particles will be seen.

If there is good reason to believe that the *disease really is smallpox*, then specimens must be taken under prescribed conditions and sent to a laboratory that is licensed to handle this virus by the Dangerous Pathogens Committee where further tests, including gel diffusion tests and the inoculation of the chorioallantoic membrane of fertile eggs will be carried out.

Incidence

The last "natural" case of smallpox occurred in Somalia on October 26, 1977. The last two outbreaks in Britain have been due to laboratory-acquired infection.

Notification

Notify the M.O.E.H. on first suspecting the diagnosis.

Incubation period

Up to 17 days.

Isolation

Preliminary—see Exotic Diseases (p. 23).

Final—the M.O.E.H. will see the patient wherever he is (do not move him but list all his contacts if in the surgery, *etc.*) and it is his duty, if he considers the diagnosis likely to be smallpox, to arrange for the transport of the patient by special ambulance to a designated smallpox hospital.

Period of infectivity

Probably until all crusts have disappeared.

Disinfection

Terminal disinfection of homes, wards, ambulances and premises must be carried out.

School exclusion

Until clinically well after release from designated hospital.

Contacts

Close contacts (household, near workers, *etc.*, or those having contact with the patient's blood or discharges, or handling the patient's corpse) should be listed, vaccinated and kept under surveillance for 16 days from the date of the last exposure. If the temperature remains normal and there is no sign of illness, no restriction of movement is necessary. If pyrexia or other sign of smallpox occurs, admit to special hospital.

Cause and epidemiology

During the 18th and 19th centuries the disease was common in Britain and it persisted until the middle 1930s. Since then all outbreaks apart from laboratory acquired infections have been due to imported cases. True smallpox only affects man naturally and spread is through case to case transmission or *via* fomites; as the smallpox virus is extremely resistant it is often spread by inanimate objects. There are one or two viruses that resemble smallpox (Yoruba, monkeypox) but case to case transmission does not appear to occur in humans.

Prevention

1. Vaccination.

   Vaccination of the general public is no longer desirable and the sooner vaccination ceases to be a condition of entry to certain countries the better. In Britain the only persons who should be vaccinated against smallpox are those who work in establishments where smallpox virus is handled.

2. Procedures.

Prompt diagnosis, notification and isolation of cases, together with identification, vaccination and surveillance of all contacts will reduce the chances of secondary cases occurring.

Treatment

This will be carried out in the designated hospital and may include the use of virucidal drugs such as methisazone, antivaccinal serum and of antibiotics should secondary bacterial infection occur.

N.B. The D.H.S.S. Memorandum on the Control of Outbreaks of Smallpox, H.M.S.O. (1975) should be consulted.

LASSA FEVER *Notifiable*

Clinical presentation

1. Patients arriving in this country with diagnosed Lassa fever. These will be sent directly to a designated hospital.
2. Patients arriving from West Africa suffering from an unexplained pyrexia. These patients should attend a designated centre for tropical diseases even if Lassa fever is not suspected.

    Neither of the above categories is likely to involve the general practitioner.
3. Laboratory workers at institutes where this virus is handled.
4. Patients from West Africa who develop unexplained pyrexia within 24 days of arriving in this country.

Investigations

1. Malaria must be excluded; specimens should be taken and examined under safe conditions by the physician in charge of the case or a consultant microbiologist.
2. If there are still grounds for suspicion, the M.O.E.H. should call in an expert in tropical medicine.
3. If the latter believes there are grounds for suspecting Lassa fever the M.O.E.H. must arrange transport and admission to a designated hospital.

Incidence

Only two known cases have so far arrived in this country.

Notification

The M.O.E.H. must be notified on suspicion as an emergency; further action must be carried out only after consultation with him.

Incubation period

3 to 21 days for control purposes.

Isolation

1. Preliminary—see Exotic Diseases (p. 23).
2. Hospital—the patient will be nursed in a designated high security containment unit.

Period of infectivity

Not known for certain, but probably fairly short (7 to 14 days).

Disinfection

Terminal disinfection of home, ward, ambulance and premises must be carried out.

School exclusion

Until clinically well and following discharge from special hospital.

Contacts

Close contacts (household contacts, near workers, *etc.*, or those having contact with the patient's blood, urine, *etc.*, or those handling a patient's personal belongings or coming into contact with a patient's corpse) should be listed and kept under surveillance for 21 days from the last date of exposure. As long as the temperature remains normal there should be no restriction of movement but a rise in temperature or signs or symptoms at all suggestive of this infection should indicate immediate isolation and consideration of admission to a designated hospital.

Cause and epidemiology

The disease is caused by an arenavirus, related to that causing lymphocytic choriomeningitis. The symptoms are not very specific but the onset is usually insidious and the symptoms include sore throat, headache, cough, vomiting, myalgia, diarrhoea and pain in the chest or abdomen. Throat ulcers, lymphadenopathy, conjunctivitis and swelling of the face and neck appear later.

The disease first appeared in Nigeria in 1969. It has since occurred in Sierra Leone and Liberia; serological surveys suggest it occurs also in Guinea and the Central African Republic. The usual sequence of events is that a case occurring in the community is admitted to hospital where it becomes the centre of an outbreak involving doctors and nurses. The mortality of such outbreaks is about 35% but tertiary cases are rare. Serological tests show that there are in the community many mild or subclinical cases, so that the overall mortality is quite low. The only animal so far to be shown to carry the virus is the ubiquitous multimammate mouse, but its importance as a vector remains to be determined.

Prevention

1. General.
    No vaccine is at present available and only a high level of hospital hygiene is likely to control the infection in such institutions; unfortunately the disease occurs in areas where this is difficult to achieve.

2. In Britain.

Prompt notification of the M.O.E.H. of suspected cases will allow precautionary measures to be taken early and reduce the probability of secondary cases arising.

Treatment

The only specific treatment at present is the administration of serum from patients recovered from the infection.

The D.H.S.S. Memorandum on Lassa Fever, H.M.S.O. (1976) should be consulted.

EBOLA FEVER, MARBURG DISEASE   *Notifiable*

Clinical presentation

1. Patients arriving in this country suffering from diagnosed Ebola fever or Marburg disease. These will go directly to a designated hospital.
2. Patients arriving from the Sudan, Zaire or other areas where these diseases are known to occur suffering from an unexplained pyrexia. These patients should attend a designated centre for tropical diseases even when Ebola fever or Marburg disease is not suspected.

    Neither of the above categories is likely to involve the general practitioner.
3. Laboratory workers in institutes where these viruses are handled.
4. Patients from the Sudan, Zaire or other areas where these diseases occur developing an unexplained pyrexia within 24 days of arrival in Britain.

Investigations

1. Malaria must be excluded; specimens should be taken and examined under safe conditions by the physician in charge of the case or a consultant microbiologist.
2. If there are still grounds for suspicion, the M.O.E.H. should call in an expert in tropical medicine.
3. If the latter thinks there are grounds for suspecting Ebola fever or Marburg disease the M.O.E.H. must arrange transport and admission to a designated hospital.

Incidence

Only one case of Ebola infection has occurred in this country and this was through accidental self inoculation by a laboratory worker.

Notification

The M.O.E.H. must be notified on suspicion; further action must be carried out only after consultation with him.

Incubation period

3 to 21 days for control purposes.

Isolation

1. Preliminary—see Exotic Diseases (p. 23).

2. Hospital—the patient will be nursed in a designated high security containment unit.

Period of infectivity

Patients have been found to be infectious up to 7 weeks from the onset.

Disinfection

Terminal disinfection of home, ward, ambulance and premises must be carried out.

School exclusion

Until clinically well and pronounced no longer infectious by the M.O.E.H.

Contacts

Close contacts (household contacts, near workers, *etc.*, or those having contact with the patient's blood, urine, *etc.*, or those handling a patient's personal belongings or coming into contact with a patient's corpse) should be listed and kept under surveillance for 21 days from the last date of exposure. As long as the temperature remains normal there should be no restriction of movement but a rise in temperature or signs or symptoms at all suggestive of these infections should indicate immediate isolation and consideration of admission to a designated hospital.

Cause and epidemiology

The viruses that cause these infections are similar in appearance but serologically distinct. Marburg disease first occurred in the town of that name and in Frankfurt and Yugoslavia in 1967 as a result of the arrival at biological institutions in those towns of a batch of green monkeys infected with the virus. There were 31 human cases and 7 deaths. In 1975 a man who had hitchiked through Rhodesia developed the disease and died in South Africa. He infected his fellow traveller and she in turn infected a nurse. In late 1976 there were large outbreaks of a similar disease in Zaire and southern Sudan, involving over 500 cases and scores of deaths; the causative organism was serologically distinct from the Marburg virus and the disease became known as Ebola fever. Later in that year a laboratory worker in England accidentally inoculated himself with the virus of Ebola fever and developed the disease but recovered.

In both diseases the onset is sudden with prostration, pains in the limbs and headache; there may be a maculopapular rash and in severe cases there is haemorrhage from many orifices of the body.

Prevention

1. General—no vaccine is available at present; in any case these diseases seem to have disappeared for the present. When they are endemic only high standards of personal hygiene can afford protection.
2. In Britain—prompt notification of the M.O.E.H. of suspected cases will allow precautionary measures to be taken early and reduce the probability of secondary cases arising.

Treatment

There is, at present, no specific treatment.

GASTROENTERITIS AND SIMILAR INFECTIONS
Notifiable, some forms

Clinical presentation
Diarrhoea and/or vomiting, sometimes with pyrexia and signs of dehydration.

Specific infectious causes
Bacterial
1. Salmonella species.
2. Shigella species.
3. Pathogenic *E. coli*.
4. *Staphylococcus aureus*.
5. *Cl. perfringens* (*welchii*).
6. *Bacillus cereus*.
7. *Vibrio parahaemolyticus*.
8. Campylobacter species.

Viral
9. Rotavirus.
10. Parvovirus.

Amoebic—
11. *Entamoeba histolyticus*.

N.B. There are many non-infectious causes of gastroenteritis.

Notification
Although all the above organisms are probably spread by the ingestion of contaminated food, the actual article of food or even the meal responsible may not be easily determinable. When an accurate assessment of the cause of the infection *can* be made the disease may be described as "Food poisoning" and as such is notifiable to the M.O.E.H. Infections due to shigella organisms are notifiable as "Dysentery" and cholera, which may be imported by the occasional holiday-maker returning from abroad, is also notifiable.

GASTROENTERITIS

SALMONELLA INFECTIONS *Notifiable*

Clinical presentation

Sudden onset of abdominal pain, diarrhoea, nausea and vomiting. If clusters of cases occur a common source must be suspected and enquiries about eating habits should be made.

Investigations

Faeces should be submitted (ideally three consecutive daily specimens) in a clean container; these should yield the responsible organism on culture. Food left over from suspected meals should be examined, even if it has to be rescued from the dustbin.

Incidence

About 8000 isolations from man are made annually in England and Wales.

Notification

Statutory, to the M.O.E.H., as food poisoning. The many stable serotypes of salmonella make notification very worth while, as the spread of infection may usually be followed fairly easily.

Incubation period

6 to 72 hours.

Isolation

Patients should be excluded from food handling or dealing with young children until three bacteriologically negative stools have been produced more than 24 hours after ceasing antibiotics.

Period of infectivity

This is variable and bacteriological clearance tests are needed. Antibiotic treatment appears to prolong excretion.

Disinfection

Of nappies, *etc.*, in young babies and of stools in communities where the sewage disposal system is not adequate.

School exclusion

Young children should be excluded until free from infection. Older and responsible children and adults may be allowed back to school when clinically well following discussion with the M.O.E.H.

Contacts

Early in an outbreak many contacts may need to be examined in order to determine the source and spread of the infection but when an outbreak has become established examination should be selective. Close contacts of cases should be excluded from food handling or dealing with young children until shown bacteriologically to be free from infection.

Source and epidemiology

Infection is through eating foods contaminated with salmonella organisms. These may be intrinsically present in the food, *e.g. Salm. hadar* in turkeys, or introduced into the food by the cook, *e.g. Salm. typhimurium*. There are about 1500 serotypes of salmonella of which about 150 are active each year. The commonest at present are *Salm. typhimurium*, *Salm. hadar*, *Salm. agona*, *Salm. virchow*, *Salm. heidelberg*, *Salm. enteritidis* and *Salm. indiana*.

Prevention

Hygiene in the kitchen, restaurant, shop and farm and adequate cooking. Following an institutional outbreak it is important to ensure that all foodhandlers are free from infection and to take environmental swabs to show that the organism is no longer present in the kitchens.

Treatment

Antibiotics are not indicated except where pyrexia is prolonged or where septicaemia occurs; these cases should be treated with ampicillin.

GASTROENTERITIS

SHIGELLA INFECTIONS (BACILLARY DYSENTERY)
Notifiable

Clinical presentation

1. Sporadic cases with moderate degree of diarrhoea and abdominal pain, the more severe cases passing blood and mucus in the stools.
2. Small family or larger institutional outbreaks in which the onsets of symptoms may be staggered rather than synchronous as in food poisoning.

Investigations

Culture of stools, submitted in a clean container, should yield a member of the Shigella group of organisms. Environmental swabs may be taken from toilets in nursery schools, *etc*.

Incidence

Very variable from year to year. About 10,000 isolations of *Sh. sonnei* and 500 of other types are made annually in England and Wales, but even Sonne dysentery is not common in recent years.

Notification

Statutory, to the M.O.E.H.

Incubation period

Usually less than 4 days.

Isolation

Patients should be kept at home during the acute stage.

Period of infectivity

The patient may excrete the organism for up to 4 weeks; rarely chronic carriers occur but these are not necessarily infectious.

Disinfection

Of nappies, *etc*. of young babies and of stools in communities where the sewage disposal system is not adequate.

School exclusion

Until clinically well, after discussion with the M.O.E.H.

Contacts

No action needed.

Source and epidemiology

In the United Kingdom the commonest causal organism is *Shigella sonnei* which mainly affects young children and is commonest in the winter. Acute cases with fluid stools and explosive diarrhoea appear to be the main source of infection, while symptomless excretors do not seem to be involved in the spread of infection.

Prevention

1. Exclusion from school or nursery of all acute cases of diarrhoea.
2. Supervised handwashing after toilet; use a 1 in 64 dilution of 1% benzalkonium chloride.
3. Frequent disinfection of toilet seats, handles and door handles.
4. Provision of disposable paper towels.

In the past such precautions as these have usually served merely to slow down the passage of infection through the institution.

Treatment

Not usually needed. Only fluids should be given by mouth until diarrhoea ceases. Antibiotics or sulphonamides are rarely needed and should certainly not be used routinely.

GASTROENTERITIS

PATHOGENIC *ESCH. COLI* INFECTIONS
Not notifiable

Clinical presentation

A disease of young babies mainly in institutions, often in the form of small outbreaks. The diarrhoea is often accompanied by severe dehydration.

Investigations

Specimens of faeces, in a clean container, yield *Esch. coli* on culture. This may be shown to be a recognised pathogenic type by serological tests.

Incidence

About 3500 suspected enteropathogenic types of *Esch. coli* are isolated annually from children under 3 with diarrhoea in England and Wales; it is probable that only a small proportion of these are responsible for the patient's clinical condition. Serious outbreaks in maternity units, special baby units, *etc.* no longer seem common.

Notification

There is no statutory requirement for notification but the M.O.E.H. will be grateful to hear of outbreaks.

Incubation period

One day or less.

Isolation

Acute cases disseminate the organism widely and must be strictly isolated.

Period of infectivity

Until bacteriologically free from infection.

Disinfection

Soiled napkins, *etc.* and the whole environment of an acute case should be disinfected.

School exclusion

Does not apply.

Contacts

Stools of ward staff should be examined and any staff carrying the infecting serotype should be given duties away from young babies. Babies in the same ward should have their stools examined and an attempt should be made to segregate or discharge any carriers of the epidemic strain.

Source and epidemiology

Esch. coli, the common coliform organism of the human gut, comprises a large number of stable serotypes (*cf.* salmonella). Some of these are occasional pathogens and may be introduced into a ward or nursery and spread widely among the babies. A few of these develop acute diarrhoea and their stools consist of an almost pure culture of the offending organism, so that the surrounding environment is rapidly and heavily contaminated. Infection appears to be achieved by a small number of organisms. The pathogenicity of even the known "enteropathogenic" types is very variable.

Prevention

1. Breast feeding.
2. "Rooming in"—the baby stays in mother's room and is kept away from the communal nursery.
3. Prompt isolation of acute cases.
4. Environmental hygiene, especially handwashing before handling babies.
5. Quarantine of babies admitted to hospital until shown to be free from pathogens.

Treatment

This should be directed mainly to fluid replacement; antibiotics are not indicated.

STAPHYLOCOCCAL FOOD POISONING *Notifiable*

Clinical presentation
Acute onset of vomiting, perhaps in several persons, soon after a meal. Although the vomiting only lasts a few hours it may be very severe and the patient will feel weak for 24 hours or so.

Investigations
Vomit, stools and suspected food should be submitted for culture. It is sometimes possible to detect staphylococci in the offending food by direct microscopy.

Incidence
Very common in hot weather; single cases and small outbreaks are rarely investigated or reported.

Notification
Statutory, to the M.O.E.H.

Incubation period
2 to 4 hours.

Isolation
Not needed.

Period of infectivity
The patient is not infectious—the condition is an intoxication, not an infection.

Disinfection
Not especially indicated.

School exclusion
Until clinically well.

Contacts
Swabs should be taken from the nose and skin and any septic lesions on any food handlers involved.

Cause and epidemiology
Certain strains of *Staphylococcus aureus* produce an enterotoxin that

causes severe vomiting. These organisms may be in the nose or on the hands of a healthy carrier or may be present in pyogenic lesions. The organisms are transferred from the hands to the food and if the ambient temperature is high they will multiply rapidly and produce a large amount of toxin. These organisms are salt resistant, so that ham is a not uncommon vehicle.

Prevention

Hygiene in the kitchen and the adequate provision and use of refrigerators.

Treatment

Although the patient may appear very ill during the acute attack, most of the toxin is rapidly vomited and recovery is usually prompt. Fluids only should be taken for about 24 hours.

CL. PERFRINGENS (CL. WELCHII) FOOD POISONING
Notifiable

Clinical presentation

Begins with a colicky abdominal pain which may last for some time before the diarrhoea occurs; the latter is rarely severe and the illness is usually mild.

Investigations

Specimens of faeces and of suspected food are cultured anaerobically for the heat resistant variety of type A *Cl. perfringens*.

Incidence

Quite common among institutional eaters; the condition is often so mild as not to be recognised as food poisoning. The majority of cases are neither recognised nor notified.

Notification

Statutory, to the M.O.E.H.

Incubation period

12 to 24 hours.

Isolation

Not needed.

Period of infectivity

The patient is not infective in the ordinary sense of the word.

Disinfection

Not especially indicated.

School exclusion

Until clinically well.

Contacts

No action needed.

Cause and epidemiology

Cl. perfringens is present in the dust, soil, on floors, in the gut of man and animals and in uncooked meat. It is an anaerobe so that, when present in the centre of a large joint of meat or a deep vat of cooling gravy or stew it can proliferate and produce toxin as long as the temperature is favourable. The food poisoning variety is able to withstand boiling for up to 4 hours. This type of food poisoning affects larger catering units where large joints are cooked rather than the home where large joints can rarely be afforded at the present time.

Prevention

Hygiene in the kitchen; stockpots should not be used and large joints should be allowed to cool rapidly at room temperature and then immediately refrigerated. Maintenance of food at 25 to 35°C should be avoided.

Treatment

Rarely needed.

GASTROENTERITIS

BACILLUS CEREUS **FOOD POISONING**   *Notifiable*

Clinical presentation
Acute vomiting follows a meal, often containing fried rice, and in about 3 hours diarrhoea follows. The disease is usually mild, but may occasionally be serious and fatalities have occurred.

Investigations
Bacteriological examination of vomit, stools and suspected food.

Incidence
Probably fairly common but only large outbreaks are usually invesitgated.

Notification
Statutory, to the M.O.E.H.

Incubation period
1. From fried rice—1 to 2 hours.
2. From other foods—about 10 hours.

Isolation
Not needed.

Period of infectivity
The patient is not infective.

Disinfection
Not especially needed.

School exclusion
Until clinically well.

Contacts
No action needed.

Cause and epidemiology
Bacillus cereus is present in soil, water and dust and is a common food contaminant. Its spores survive cooking, and as the food cools to below 40°C the organism begins to multiply and produce toxin. Outbreaks are often associated with the eating of fried rice which is

44

usually prepared by leaving cold boiled rice overnight and gently frying it as needed; fresh boiled rice is no problem. Other vehicles include vegetables, meat dishes and sauces.

Prevention

Kitchen hygiene, especially the rapid cooling, followed by refrigeration, of all cooked food.

Treatment

Rarely needed, but in severe cases should be directed towards fluid replacement.

GASTROENTERITIS

VIBRIO PARAHAEMOLYTICUS **FOOD POISONING**
Notifiable

Clinical presentation
A colicky abdominal pain with watery diarrhoea, often with vomiting, headache and fever. A moderately severe illness lasting 1 to 7 days.

Investigations
Cultures from stools and offending shellfish yield growth of *V. parahaemolyticus*.

Incidence
Uncommon in Britain. It occurs mainly in Japan and U.S.A.

Notification
Statutory, to the M.O.E.H.

Incubation period
12 to 24 hours.

Isolation
Not needed.

Period of infectivity
The patient is not infectious.

Disinfection
Not especially indicated.

School exclusion
Until clinically well.

Contacts
No action needed.

Cause and epidemiology
V. parahaemolyticus is a marine vibrio living in marine silt; as the water gets warmer in summer the vibrio leaves the silt, passes into the water and becomes a common contaminant of fish and shellfish, particularly in tropical and subtropical waters. Heavily contami-

nated seafood which is left at ambient temperature for any length of time will yield sufficient numbers of vibrios as to cause illness.

Prevention

Sterilisation or refrigeration of exotic seafood.

Treatment

Rarely needed apart from dietetic advice.

CAMPYLOBACTER INFECTION *Not notifiable*

Clinical presentation

A period of pyrexia and malaise lasting about 24 hours is followed by diarrhoea, the stools becoming progressively watery; in some cases faecal incontinence may occur. There is often severe abdominal pain and sometimes indications of bacteraemia. Recovery may be slow and there may be a marked loss of weight.

Investigations

Stools submitted during the acute stage yield campylobacter on selective media and blood cultures may also be positive. Specific antibodies appear early in the infection.

Incidence

Campylobacter is at present the commonest identifiable cause of infectious diarrhoea, about 6% of all cases of diarrhoea being caused by this organism.

Notification

As the infection rarely manifests itself as obvious food poisoning notification is not often statutory but the M.O.E.H. will be glad to be informed of outbreaks as soon as possible.

Incubation period

2 to 10 days; it is very variable, even within an outbreak, so that cases emerge over a period of over a week.

Isolation

Not needed, but food handling should be forbidden at least during the acute phase of the illness.

Period of infectivity

Not yet known for certain.

Disinfection

Of stools in areas where the sewage disposal system is not adequate.

School exclusion

Until clinically well.

Contacts

No action needed.

Cause and epidemiology

The infection is caused by members of the Campylobacter group of organisms (formerly the *Vibrio fetus* group). Infection is contracted by the ingestion of contaminated food. The organism multiplies in the small bowel and may invade the bloodstream. The types of food mainly implicated have not yet been determined but the organism is widespread in the poultry population and outbreaks have followed the eating of chicken. Young dogs are frequently infected. A large outbreak followed the contamination of the public water supply. About 1% of the population are symptomless carriers.

Prevention

By kitchen hygiene, especially adequate cooking, refrigeration and personal hygiene.

Treatment

For septicaemia, gentamycin, 80 mg should be given intramuscularly 4 times a day in adults; children need 4 mg/kg daily in 3 divided doses. If the diarrhoea is severe adults should be given 500 mg erythromycin 4 times a day; children 10 to 20 kg need 125 mg 6-hourly and bigger children 250 mg 6-hourly.

GASTROENTERITIS

ROTAVIRUS INFECTION   *Not notifiable*

Clinical presentation

Sudden onset of vomiting in children under 5 years of age is followed after 2 to 3 days by the passage of loose yellow-green offensive stools. The illness is usually mild, lasting 5 to 8 days.

Investigations

The virus may be detected in stools taken early in the illness on examination by electron microscopy.

Incidence

Very common—it accounts for 40 to 50% of all gastroenteritis in children aged 6 months to 6 years.

Notification

Not needed.

Incubation period

2 to 3 days.

Isolation

Not usually practicable.

Period of infectivity

Not known for certain but probably short—about a week.

Disinfection

Of stools and contaminated clothing, napkins, *etc*.

School exclusion

Not usually applicable, but in older children until clinically well.

Contacts

No action needed.

Cause and epidemiology

The rotavirus (synonyms: orbivirus, reo-like virus) is so called because of a vague resemblance to a wheel. It is related to viruses causing infectious diarrhoea in calves and other animals. It is a disease of cooler months, rarely affecting patients outside the limits of 6 months to 6 years.

Prevention

It is a disease of institutions and its spread in paediatric wards is impossible to control.

Treatment

Rarely needed but fluid replacement is important, especially in younger patients.

PARVOVIRUS GASTROENTERITIS *Notifiable only as food poisoning*

Clinical presentation

These "small round" viruses may be associated with winter vomiting disease in which outbreaks of severe vomiting occur among mainly young children in schools, hostels, *etc*. They have also been found in the stools of patients suffering from food poisoning caused by cockles. There is usually severe vomiting for 6 to 12 hours with little diarrhoea and a surprisingly rapid recovery. In outbreaks caused by cockles there have been secondary cases in the affected households in persons who did not eat the shellfish.

Investigations

The virus may be detected by electronmicroscopy after it has been purified from the stools using gradient centrifugation.

Incidence

Probably quite common but rarely diagnosed as sporadic cases and small outbreaks are not investigated and few laboratories have the time and facilities to investigate fully.

Notification

When occurring as food poisoning—to the M.O.E.H.

Incubation period

As food poisoning, less than 24 hours; for winter vomiting disease 2 to 7 days.

Isolation

Not needed.

Period of infectivity

Probably a few days only.

Disinfection

Not especially indicated.

School exclusion

Until clinically well.

Contacts

No action needed.

Cause and epidemiology

Small viruses, about 26 nm in diameter, have been found in outbreaks of gastroenteritis all over the world. There are several serological types—Norwalk, Montgomerie, Hawaii, *etc.*

Prevention

Adequate cooking and prevention of contamination of shellfish from sewage. Shellfish should not be gathered from polluted water.

Treatment

Rarely needed except for the replacement of fluids.

AMOEBIC DYSENTERY   *Notifiable*

Clinical presentation

Diarrhoea with insidious onset followed by remissions and relapses. There is usually a history of residence in an endemic area (including the U.S.A.) and there may be evidence of liver involvement.

Investigations

Amoebae may be seen by direct microscopical examination of the stools from acute cases or from chronic cases in relapse. The microscope should be brought to the bedside and specimens obtained by sigmoidoscopy. In chronic cases and carriers only cysts may be usually seen. Fluorescent antibody tests usually give low positive results in chronic cases; this may merely indicate previous infection. Cases with liver abscess usually give levels of about 1 in 200.

Incidence

Practically all cases occurring in Britain have been contracted abroad; about 200 cases occur here annually. The carrier rate throughout the world is said to vary between 0·2 and 50%; it must be low in this country.

Notification

Statutory, to the M.O.E.H.

Incubation period

3 weeks to 3 months.

Isolation

Not needed but patients should be excluded from food handling.

Period of infectivity

Probably years in chronic cases and carriers.

Disinfection

Of stools in places where sewage disposal is not adequate.

School exclusion

Until clinically well.

Contacts

No action needed.

Cause and epidemiology

Caused by *Entamoeba histolytica*. Patients contract the disease by eating food contaminated by cysts from the faeces of carriers or chronic cases. In the small intestine the cyst wall is ruptured and an amoeba is liberated which gives rise to four trophozooites. These pass to the large bowel where they produce flask shaped ulcers in the sigmoidorectal region.

Treatment

Acute cases—metronidazole (Flagyl) 800 mg 3 times a day for 10 days. Carriers and chronic cases should receive metronidazole 800 mg 3 times a day for 3 days followed by diloxanide furoate (Furamide) 20 mg/kg/day for 10 days.

Prevention

The screening of food handlers in tropical countries and the prompt diagnosis and treatment of cases and carriers; avoidance of uncooked unwashed fruit and salads in areas where the carrier rate is high.

N.B. Amoebic dysentery frequently mimics colitis so that, before suspected cases of colitis are treated with surgery or steroids, stools should be examined, biopsy carried out and serological tests done to exclude amoebiasis.

VIRAL HEPATITIS

TYPE A HEPATITIS (INFECTIOUS HEPATITIS)
Notifiable

Clinical presentation

A mild to moderate jaundice is preceded by anorexia and vague general illness. The stools are light in colour and the urine is dark. There is no suggestion of a surgical cause and there are no markers of type B hepatitis in the serum.

Investigations

Paired sera show an increase in level of antibodies to hepatitis A virus as detected by radioimmunoassay or other tests. Liver function tests may determine the severity of liver damage and the rate of recovery.

Specimens should be labelled "High risk", sealed in a plastic bag and accompanied by a separate form.

Incidence

A very common infection. Although in young people the infection usually causes clinical illness, most infections are symptomless.

Notification

Statutory, to the M.O.E.H.

Incubation period

3 to 5 weeks.

Isolation

Not needed.

Period of infectivity

The virus disappears from the stools when jaundice appears.

Disinfection

Not especially indicated.

School exclusion

Until clinically well.

Contacts

Young people who are close contacts should be excluded from work for 6 weeks if they are food handlers or deal with young children. Child contacts need not normally be excluded from school.

Cause and epidemiology

The disease is contracted by eating contaminated food or drinking water polluted by sewage. Viraemia is transient so that the blood is rarely infective. The only target organ is the liver and biopsy shows severe damage during the acute stage of the disease although complete recovery almost always occurs.

Prevention

As the virus will have disappeared from the stools when jaundice appears, isolation of the patient plays no part in prevention of spread. A clean water supply is the most important factor in the prophylaxis and good personal hygiene is second; in hospitals for the mentally subnormal, where personal hygiene is at its lowest, the disease flourishes.

Travellers to countries where the water supply is suspect and where the disease is common may be protected for about 3 months by the injection of 750 mg of normal human immunoglobulin.

Treatment

There is no specific treatment.

VIRAL HEPATITIS

TYPE B HEPATITIS (SERUM JAUNDICE) *Notifiable*

Clinical presentation

There is moderate to severe jaundice with no obvious surgical or toxic cause. The stools are light in colour and the urine dark. The patient may have been exposed parenterally to blood or blood products over 6 weeks earlier.

Investigations

Hepatitis B surface antigen is usually detected in the serum by reverse passive haemagglutination, radioimmunoassay or electron microscopy. Other markers are sometimes sought—surface antibody, core antibody, e antigen and antibody and DNA polymerase.

Specimens must be labelled "High Risk", sealed in a plastic bag and accompanied by a separate form.

Incidence

About 1600 new cases and 1000 new carriers are detected each year in England and Wales. In the U.K. about 0·1% of the population are carriers, but in the middle and far east up to 10% are, while in Iceland up to 30% are said to be.

Notification

Infective jaundice is statutorily notifiable to the M.O.E.H., so that cases are notifiable but carriers are not.

Incubation period

2 to 30 weeks; rarely less than 6 weeks.

Isolation

Not needed.

Period of infectivity

Acute cases usually become noninfective within a few weeks, but in a few cases the jaundice is mild and recurrent and the patient becomes a carrier. This state may persist for years.

Disinfection

Of blood or bloodstained discharges, *etc.*

58

School exclusion
Until clinically well.

Contacts
The disease sometimes appears in the form of small outbreaks among drug addicts and male homosexuals, so that contact tracing and testing among spouses and heterosexual and homosexual partners may be useful. All blood used for transfusion in Britain is now tested for surface antigen so that the disease rarely follows transfusion.

Cause and epidemiology
The disease is caused by a virus unlike any other known which consists of a core—the virus particle—and a large capsule. The complete virus is known as a Dane body, and these may be visualised using electron microscopy; in most cases there is an excess of capsular material in the serum in the form of circular bodies and rods. Within infected liver cells the virus has no capsule. Thus, there are at least 2 antigens—surface (capsule) antigen and core (virus particle) antigen. Similarly there are two antibodies produced, core and surface antibody.

Infection is always contracted from another human case or carrier by means of blood (perhaps also semen or saliva). In straightforward cases the virus appears in the blood about a month after infection and the blood remains infectious until convalescence is over. A few people remain carriers for an indefinite period; some of these are healthy carriers but many show a persistent hepatic lesion that may become progressive.

The risk is greatest through accidental inoculation from an infected needle, drug abuse, tattooing, acupuncture, injections made using the same needle or syringe for more than one person, in dialysis units and among male homosexuals.

Prevention
1. Screening of all units of blood issued for transfusion.
2. Prompt and correct disposal of used syringes in puncture proof boxes or tins.
3. Education of medical, nursing and laboratory staff in the dangers of blood born infection.
4. Education of drug-takers and male homosexuals in the dangers inherent in their habits.
5. Where exposure has occurred, *e.g.* a known hepatitis B surface antigen negative laboratory worker accidentally pricks himself or

herself with a needle contaminated with blood from a known HBsAg positive patient, specific hepatitis B immunoglobulin may be administered. This may be obtained from the Central Public Health Laboratory, Colindale, or through the local Public Health Laboratory.

6. Babies born to women suffering from type B hepatitis at the time of delivery should also receive specific immunoglobulin.

LEPTOSPIRAL INFECTION (WEIL'S DISEASE)
Notifiable

Clinical presentation

The disease takes the form of an acute septicaemia which gives rise to acute febrile illness with severe muscle pain; at this stage diagnosis is almost impossible unless the patient's occupation gives a clue. In more severe cases target organs, particularly the liver, kidney and meninges are attacked and the onset of jaundice gives an indication of the cause. Death may result from renal failure.

Investigations

There is usually a marked polymorphonuclear leucocytosis and casts, and white cells are present in the urine. In the early stages the organism may be cultured from the blood and *fresh alkaline* urine and may also be seen using a darkground microscope. Antibody appears during the first week and reaches a high level after 3 weeks. In acutely fatal cases the organism may be seen in and cultured from ground up kidney or liver tissue.

Notification

It may be notified to the M.O.E.H. as "Infectious jaundice" but is also notifiable under the Industrial Injuries Scheme when probably contracted at work.

Incubation period

3 to 15 days, usually about 10 days.

Isolation

Not needed.

Period of infectivity

Case-to-case spread does not occur.

Disinfection

Not especially indicated.

School exclusion

Until clinically well.

Contacts

Those sharing the patient's exposure should be kept under surveillance for a few days for their own good.

Incidence

About 50 cases annually in Britain.

Cause and epidemiology

Due to infection by *Leptospira icterohaemorrhagiae* and related spirochaetes. This organism is carried by the common rat and man may become infected by contaminated rat urine. Immersion in rat infested water or drunken repose in a damp ditch frequently figure in the patient's history. *L. canicola* is carried by dogs and causes meningitis rather than jaundice.

Prevention

Any procedure likely to eliminate rats would be expected to reduce the incidence of Weil's disease. Workers in sewers and other places with a high rat population should wear protective clothing including rubber boots and gloves. Vaccines are in use overseas but there is no available information as to their efficiency.

Treatment

Although penicillin may be of doubtful use few would dare to withhold it as the organism is very sensitive; perhaps its use as a prophylactic in contacts would appear more logical. In spite of the often dramatic jaundice treatment should be directed towards remedying the less apparent renal failure.

Clinical presentation
1. Congenital—onset 6 to 21 days from delivery:
   a. Generalised illness with rash, purpura, jaundice, enlarged liver and spleen—usually fatal.
   b. Localised form with only a few vesicles—usually mild.
2. Acquired:
   a. Stomatitis—the commonest form of primary infection, occurring mainly in children under the age of 6 years.
   b. Herpetic whitlow.
   c. Primary ocular herpes.
   d. Primary genital herpes—often in the form of vulvovaginitis.
   e. Recurrent herpes—may occur in all the above sites following primary infection at or near that site.
   f. Herpetic meningoencephalitis—usually a grave illness.

Investigations
1. Vesicles—a drop of sterile distilled water is placed on the vesicle and the vesicle is opened with a pointed scalpel; the mixture of vesicle fluid and water is taken up by capillary tubes, both ends of which are subsequently plugged with plasticene; the tubes are placed in a screw-capped glass container (universal container) for transport; using the scalpel scrape the base of the vesicle and apply the scrapings to several positions on an etched slide—these will be used for fluorescent antibody tests; finally take a swab of the base of the vesicle and submit in virus transport medium for tissue culture.
2. Serology—only at the time of the primary infection may an increase in specific complement fixing antibody be demonstrated between acute and convalescent serum.
3. In herpes encephalitis a brain biopsy may show herpes-like viruses on electron microscopy.

Incidence
Universal; most people are infected in childhood but a few escape until early adult life.

Notification
None required.

Incubation period
Up to 2 weeks.

Isolation
Not required.

Period of infectivity
As long as vesicles are present.

Disinfection
Not especially indicated.

School exclusion
Only as long as there is secondary impetiginous infection of the lesion.

Contacts
The disease is serious in small or eczematous babies so that nurses or other attendants with lesions of the skin or the hands should be given other duties until the lesions have healed.

Cause and epidemiology
Primary infection usually occurs in childhood and is contracted from another human case; after this lesion has healed the virus remains dormant, probably in the posterior root ganglia (*cf* varicella) and emerges to produce localised vesicles after an immunological insult, *e.g.* a cold or other infection.

There are 2 serological types: type 1 causes mainly skin and mouth lesions and type 2 mainly genital or cerebral lesions, although these distinctions seem less fixed than formerly.

Prevention
Keep suspected infections away from young babies and eczematous children.

If a woman suffering from active genital herpes infection goes into labour it is advisable to deliver by Caesarian section provided that the membranes have not been ruptured for more than 4 hours.

Treatment
Treatment is usually needed only by the compromised patient, in encephalitis and in the rare severe congenital cases.
1. Severe generalised infection—cytarabine, 10 to 13 mg/m^2/day by continuous intravenous infusion.

2. Skin lesions—10% idoxuridine in dimethyl sulphoxide.
3. Herpetic keratitis—idoxuridine is used first but if either viral resistance or patient sensitivity occur trifluorthymazine should be used.

Clinical presentation

Any pyrexial illness or CNS disturbance in a patient returning from a malarial area should be considered as malaria until disproved. The typical illness consists of headache, pyrexia and a cyclic pattern of rigours and sweating, but severe cases may present with continuous pyrexia, jaundice, shock, coagulation defects, coma, disorientation and delirium. In these severe cases it is essential that the diagnosis is made early as treatment may be life-saving.

Investigations

Thick and thin films should be examined for malarial parasites, repeatedly if necessary.

Incidence

Although the disease has been pretty well eliminated from Europe and the Americas, in those developing countries where there has been no prolonged period of peace to allow of environmental improvement, as in central Africa, the disease is as easily acquired as in the days of Livingstone. Malaria is rarely contracted in Britain although one case recently occurred in Holland in a patient living near the airport and there was a small outbreak in the Essex marshes shortly after the first world war. During the nineteenth century the disease ("the ague") appears to have been quite common in Britain.

Notification

Statutory—to the M.O.E.H.

Incubation period

Usually 12 to 30 days.

Isolation

Not needed.

Period of infectivity

Cases occurring in Britain are not infectious, as the correct mosquito vector is absent.

Disinfection
Not especially indicated.

School exclusion
Until clinically well.

Contacts
No action normally needed, but it might be worth while to make sure that persons who have shared the pertinent holiday with a case have continued with suppressive treatment on return.

Cause and epidemiology
Plasmodium falciparum causes malignant malaria and most malarial deaths in this country are caused by this organism. *Plasmodium vivax, malariae* and *ovale* cause less severe infections but the first has a tendency to recur. Infection is contracted through the bite of an infected mosquito and sporozoites from the insect's saliva pass through the bloodstream to the liver; here cells are parasitised and the organism passes through several cycles of reproduction, invading more and more liver cells. After this exoerythrocytic phase, a red cell becomes parasitised: the parasite enlarges and divides into a number of merozoites; the red cell ruptures and each merozoite invades another red cell. At this stage the symptoms of infection commence and, as the early cycles of red cell invasion are synchronous, a cyclical pyrexia begins the symptoms, but later the invasion cycles get out of step and the pyrexia is continuous.

Prevention
1. Suppressive drugs: chloroquin, 300 mg weekly should be taken while in a malarious area. On returning a daily dose of 15 mg primaquin should be taken for 14 days, as chloroquin does not kill the organisms in the liver.
2. Mosquito nets and insect repellant (*e.g.* dimethylphthallate) should be used when indicated.
3. Efforts should be made by the local authorities to reduce the mosquito population.

Treatment
1. All infections (except *P. falciparum* contracted in South America or Southeast Asia):
   Chloroquin—600 mg immediately, 300 mg 6 hours later and 300 mg daily for 2 to 5 days.

2. *P. falciparum* infections contracted in South America or in Southeast Asia:

   Quinine sulphate or hydrochloride—650 mg 8 hourly for 3 days then 12 hourly for 7 days (15 g in 10 days) *also* pyrimethamine—25 mg twice a day for 3 days.

Clinical presentation

This acute fever of childhood is characterised by a prodromal period of a few days during which the child may appear quite ill, followed by a characteristic rash appearing on the face and spreading to the rest of the body. Coryza and conjunctivitis are common symptoms. Koplik's spots are present on the buccal mucosa near the molar teeth and may be useful in diagnosing the infection before the rash has appeared or in dark skinned subjects.

Secondary bacterial infections such as bronchitis or middle ear disease are not uncommon.

Investigations

Few cases require laboratory confirmation.

A mouth swab in virus transport medium should yield the virus in tissue culture. Paired sera will show a rise of specific complement fixing or haemagglutination inhibiting antibody.

Incidence

This was formerly a very common disease, 90% of people having been infected before the age of 18. However the use of attenuated live vaccine is bound to affect the prevalence of the disease in coming years.

Notification

Statutory, to the M.O.E.H.

Incubation period

Usually 8 to 13 days.

Isolation

Keep away from other children as far as possible until 4 to 5 days after the onset of the rash.

Period of infectivity

From the beginning of the prodromal illness until about 4 days after the appearance of the rash.

Disinfection

Not especially indicated.

School exclusion

Until clinically well.

Contacts

No action needed.

Cause and epidemiology

The virus is contracted from other human cases, probably mainly during their prodromal illnesses. The virus multiplies in the upper respiratory tract and then invades the blood stream; the main target organ is the skin but the lungs may be involved. A small number of cases are followed, after months or years, by subacute sclerosing panencephalitis, resulting in deterioration and death within a few months.

Prevention

Live attenuated vaccine should be given as soon as possible after the first birthday. In children with a history of convulsions or epilepsy, chronic heart or lung disease or underdevelopment, the complications of vaccination may be reduced by giving a small dose of normal immunoglobulin when vaccinating; this may be obtained from the M.O.E.H.

Treatment

There is no specific treatment but, in view of the serious nature of some of the bacterial complications, antibiotics may be needed more frequently than in other virus infections.

Causes

Bacterial:
1. *Neisseria meningitidis*   (Meningococcal)
2. *Haemophilis influenzae*   (Influenzal)
3. *Streptococcus pneumoniae*   (Pneumococcal)

Viral:
Coxsackieviruses A and B (pp. 16, 19)   (Lymphocytic)
Echoviruses   (p. 21)   (Lymphocytic)
Mumps virus   (p. 84)   (Lymphocytic)
Herpesvirus simplex   (p. 63)   (Herpetic)
Poliovirus   (p. 13)   (Poliomyelitis)

Less common types:
4. *Mycobacterium tuberculosis*   (Tuberculous)
5. *Listeria monocytogenes*
6. *Leptospira canicola*   (Leptospiral)
7. *Naegleri fowleri*   (Amoebic)

Note

Classical cases of meningitis with neck stiffness, headache, photo-
phobia and vomiting are usually easy to diagnose. Frequently,
however, the onset of illness will be insidious and the symptoms
nonspecific. In these cases the patient will have been admitted to
hospital and the diagnosis made by performing a lumbar puncture,
often before typical clinical signs have appeared; this is particularly
the case in young babies. Thus, the possibility of definitive diagnosis
and of treatment of meningitis in general practice is not common.

MENINGOCOCCAL MENINGITIS *Notifiable*

Clinical presentation

There are usually the classical symptoms and signs of meningitis often associated with a petechial rash. Sometimes the signs of septicaemia, including the rash, precede the onset of meningitis by a few days and occasionally septicaemia occurs without meningitis.

Investigations

The cerebrospinal fluid will contain large numbers of polymorphs some containing gram negative diplococci. On culture it will yield *Neisseria meningitidis*. Nasopharyngeal or throat swabs, submitted in bacterial transport medium will yield heavy growth of the same organism and it can also be cultured from the petechial rash.

Incidence

About 400 cases per year with about 30 deaths in England and Wales.

Notification

Statutory to the M.O.E.H., as acute meningitis.

Incubation period

2 to 10 days, usually 3 or 4.

Isolation

Not strictly needed but the patient is usually nursed in an isolation block or infectious diseases hospital because of nursing expertise.

Period of infectivity

As the infecting organism is frequently found in normal throats, the patient need not be regarded as infectious in the usual sense.

Disinfection

Not especially indicated.

School exclusion

Until clinically well.

Contacts

Because of the occasional occurrence of small household outbreaks,

72

household contacts should be given prophylactic doses of sulphadimidene (2g/day for 3 days for adults) unless the strain is known to be resistant to sulphonamides when minocycline (100 mg twice a day) should be given, but not to pregnant women or children under 3 years of age.

Cause and epidemiology

Neisseria meningitidis is a fairly frequent inhabitant of the nasopharynx that, for no known reason, occasionally invades the blood stream, giving the symptoms of septicaemia, and is carried to the meninges where a purulent meningitis is produced. These cases sometimes occur in small clusters, hence the treatment of contacts. Sometimes the onset is very acute, the patient becoming comatose or manic in an hour or so and the CSF appearing quite purulent. Administration of antibiotics before the lumbar puncture is performed may sterilise the CSF and prevent specific diagnosis being made.

Prevention

See above for prophylaxis in carriers.

Vaccines—polysaccharide antigens to types A, B and C organisms have been used successfully in the U.S.A. and Finland and should obviously be used where there is a high incidence of the disease as in some parts of Africa. In Britain, although the incidence of infection is much lower than that of whooping cough, the mortality is comparable so that vaccination seems worth considering; as the majority of deaths occur in very young children the vaccine will have to be given by the end of the third month of life.

Treatment

Sulphonamides are preferred but if the organism is resistant, penicillin or parenteral ampicillin must be used.

INFLUENZAL MENINGITIS *Notifiable*

Presentation
Signs and symptoms of meningitis, usually in a child under 4 years of age.

Investigation
The CSF contains many polymorphs and a large number of gram negative bacilli. Culture yields *Haemophilus influenzae*.

Incidence
In Britain this infection is about as common as meningococcal meningitis, but in the U.S.A. it is commoner. About 400 cases and 20 deaths occur annually in Britain.

Notification
Statutory to the M.O.E.H. as acute meningitis.

Incubation period
Probably 2 to 4 days.

Isolation
The patient will usually be admitted to an isolation block or infectious diseases hospital for nursing expertise.

Period of infectivity
The patient is not infectious in the usual sense.

Disinfection
Not especially indicated.

School exclusion
Until clinically well.

Contacts
No action needed.

Cause and epidemiology
Haemophilus influenzae is a fairly common respiratory tract commensal which, for no known reason, occasionally invades the

bloodstream and thence the meninges, producing a purulent meningitis.

Prevention

There is no practical method.

Treatment

Ampicillin is given parenterally in high doses.

PNEUMOCOCCAL MENINGITIS   *Notifiable*

Clinical presentation

Signs of meningitis, usually in a child under 4 years of age; generally indistinguishable from meningitis due to other organisms.

Investigations

The CSF contains an increased number of polymorphs and gram positive cocci arranged in chains or pairs. Culture yields a profuse growth of *Streptococcus pneumoniae*.

Incidence

The infection occurs most commonly during the first year of life. In Britain there are about 250 cases each year with 10 or so deaths.

Notification

Statutory to the M.O.E.H. as acute meningitis.

Incubation period

Not known but probably a few days.

Isolation

Not needed, but the patient will usually be admitted to an isolation block or infectious disease hospital for nursing expertise.

Period of infectivity

The patient is not infectious in the ordinary sense.

Disinfection

Not especially indicated.

School exclusion

Until clinically well.

Contacts

No action needed.

Cause and epidemiology

Streptococcus pneumoniae—the pneumococcus—which caused lobar pneumonia, a common disease before the advent of antibiotics, remains as a common commensal of the respiratory tract. For no known reason it occasionally invades the bloodstream causing purulent meningitis in young children. Sometimes in older patients recurrent infection may occur; this may be due to a hairline fracture of the skull.

Prevention

Pneumococcal vaccines have been used successfully in the U.S.A. where lobar pneumonia is still prevalent. If it were used to prevent pneumococcal meningitis it would need to be administered by the end of the baby's third month.

Treatment

The organism is sensitive to penicillin which should be given intrathecally at the time of the diagnostic lumbar puncture, repeated by this route and also given in large doses by intravenous drip.

LESS COMMON FORMS OF MENINGITIS

TUBERCULOUS MENINGITIS *Notifiable*

About 30 cases are reported each year in England and Wales. The onset is usually insidious and signs of meningitis may not appear until the patient has been very ill for several days. Most cases are patients suffering from primary tuberculosis and some may be suffering from miliary tuberculosis in which the meninges are among many other organs affected. The disease should be borne in mind when dealing with immigrant children as well as contacts of tuberculous patients. Diagnosis is usually confirmed in hospital where treatment is also carried out.

LISTERIA MONOCYTOGENES MENINGITIS

About 50 cases of listeria infection are reported in England and Wales each year and in about 40% the meninges are involved. Infection is most common during the first month of life and it is probable that these cases have been infected by their mothers, probably during delivery; the organism has been shown to cause repeated abortions in infected women. The drug of choice is ampicillin and in neonatal cases the mother should be treated at the same time as the infant.

LEPTOSPIRAL MENINGITIS

Leptospira canicola may affect pigs and can be cultured from up to 40% of dogs in large cities. In humans it causes lymphocytic meningitis, the cause of which may only be established if a history of contact with a sick dog is elicited and serological tests carried out. Only one or two cases are reported each year but probably many more would be found if looked for. The disease is usually mild and self limiting in about 10 days but penicillin seems to hasten recovery.

AMOEBIC MENINGITIS

Naegleria fowleri is a free living amoeba found in stagnant water in the summer. It occasionally invades the meninges of people who swim in such water, producing a fatal meningitis. Only about 200 cases have been described throughout the world so far but several have occurred in Britain and the organism has been found in one of Britain's premier watering places where a case occurred in 1978, so that it is a cause worth considering when meningitis occurs in a bather towards the end of the summer.

OTHER ORGANISMS

It is important to remember that any organisms capable of setting up a septicaemia may reach the meninges so that staphylococci, streptococci, *E. coli*, salmonella, *Proteus, Pseudomonas* and many other organisms are repsonsible for occasional cases of meningitis each year.

MOLLUSCUM CONTAGIOSUM AND WARTS

Not notifiable

Clinical presentation

Warts often occur in numbers, especially in children. They are usually smooth and flat, covered with normal skin. On the genitalia they grow rapidly. Plantar warts are tender circular lesions with a speckled core.

Molluscum contagiosum consists of pinkish-white papules with a central pore. They are often multiple, affecting the genitalia, especially in adults.

Investigations

Laboratory confirmation is rarely needed. Sections of laryngeal papillomata from children should be examined with the electron microscope as their aetiology is similar to that of warts. Scrapings from molluscum may also be examined under the electron microscope.

Incidence

Most children develop both of these conditions at some time. Genital lesions are commonly seen in special treatment clinics.

Notification

Not notifiable

Incubation period

Warts—1 to 20 months
Molluscum—2 to 7 weeks.

Isolation

Not needed.

Period of infectivity

As long as the lesion is present.

Disinfection

Not especially indicated.

School exclusion

There is no evidence that any policy of exclusion from school or of covering the lesions have any effect on the prevalence of these conditions. Exclusion from swimming baths seems equally ineffective.

Contacts

No action needed.

Cause and epidemiology

The infections are spread by person-to-person contact, perhaps from contaminated floors or gym shoes. Genital warts are spread by sexual intercourse and are caused by a small round virus related to but not identical with that causing skin warts.

Molluscum is caused by a large virus of the poxvirus group.

Prevention

No efficient method is known.

Treatment

There is no specific treatment. Warts on the body surface may be treated with liquid nitrogen and both types of lesion on the sole of the foot may be curetted under local anaesthetic. Genital warts may be treated with 25% podophyllin in tincture of benzoin except when in pregnant women.

Both types of infection regress spontaneously.

INFECTIOUS MONONUCLEOSIS (GLANDULAR FEVER)

Not notifiable

Clinical presentation

An acute virus infection of late childhood and adolescence. The lymph nodes are enlarged, there is a sore throat, often with exudative tonsillitis, the spleen may be enlarged and there may be a fleeting rash. Mild symptoms of encephalitis are not uncommon in severe cases.

Investigations

A blood film is often diagnostic—10,000 to 20,000 white cells per mm^3, of which 15 to 20% are abnormal monocytes.

The serum usually contains antibodies that will agglutinate sheep red cells even after absorption by guinea-pig kidney to a titre of 1 in 40 or greater (Paul–Bunnell, Monospot).

The serum also contains specific antiviral antibodies that can be detected by fluorescent antibody tests; the presence of IgM or a rise in the level of IgG are both diagnostic.

Incidence

About 60% of adults possess antibody and hence have been infected.

Notification

Not needed.

Incubation period

Doubtful—probably about 14 days.

Isolation

Not needed.

Period of infectivity

Once a patient has been infected he probably remains an occasional excretor of the virus.

Disinfection

Not especially indicated.

School exclusion

Until clinically well.

Contacts

No action needed.

Cause and epidemiology

Infection is caused by the Epstein-Barr virus, one of the four viruses of the herpes family that commonly affect man. Infection occurs usually in childhood or adolescence but young children do not suffer the classical clinical effects; the infection may be symptom free or produce just a sore throat. The virus infects the lymphoid tissue, the genome becoming integrated in the genes of some lymphocytes; as they multiply the virus genetic material multiplies with them. Lymphocytes from an uninfected patient cannot be grown in tissue culture, but those from a patient recently infected by the EB virus will multiply indefinitely and the virus is excreted via the throat, probably profusely at first and becoming less as time passes. In children under 9 years of age and about 10% of adults the Paul–Bunnell test is negative and the disease must be diagnosed by looking for virus-specific antibody. Other causes of Paul–Bunnell negative glandular fever are toxoplasmosis, cytomegalovirus and adenovirus infections.

In tropical Africa the virus is associated with Burkitt's lymphoma in children.

Prevention

No method is available.

Treatment

There is no specific treatment; antibiotics should not be given as rashes occur readily in this condition and may be severe in the presence of drugs such as ampicillin.

MUMPS *Not notifiable*

Clinical presentation

This is an acute viral infection usually attacking the parotid glands, causing pain and swelling. Orchitis occurs in about 10% of men and about 5% of women suffer from oophoritis. Transient and, rarely, permanent deafness may occur, also pancreatitis, neuritis, arthritis, mastitis and pericarditis. Meningitis is not uncommon and both this condition and orchitis may occur in the absence of parotid involvement.

Investigations

Swabs should be taken from the mouth in the vicinity of Stensen's duct and submitted in virus transport medium; these should yield virus growth in tissue culture.

Two main antibodies are formed, that to the S (soluble) antigen appears very early and that to the V (virus) antigen some days later. Thus, a specimen of serum taken shortly after infection will have a high level of S antibody and little or no V antibody. Paired sera will show a rise in the level of V antibody.

Incidence

About 50% of children will have been infected before the age of 18.

Notification

Normally not notifiable, but when acute meningitis is a part of the picture the disease is statutorily notifiable to the M.O.E.H.

Incubation period

14 to 18 days.

Isolation

Keep at home, preferably away from susceptible adult males.

Period of infectivity

The patient is most infective just before the swelling occurs and may remain so for about 10 days; the virus may be present in the urine during this period.

Disinfection

Not especially indicated.

84

School exclusion

Until swelling has subsided and the patient is clinically well.

Contacts

No action needed.

Cause and epidemiology

The disease is contracted from other human cases. The virus is a myxovirus, related to the influenza viruses, and it may be acquired by droplet spread, primary replication occurring in the upper respiratory tract. It is then distributed by the blood to all parts of the body, affecting target organs such as the salivary glands, testes, CNS, *etc*. About 50% of cases are subclinical.

Prevention

A vaccine is available in the U.S.A. and it carries a 95% protection rate but it is not available in Britain.

Passive immunisation should be given to compromised patients who are contacts and to babies whose mothers develop the disease in the perinatal period by giving them specific immunoglobulin (see p. 130 for dosage).

Treatment

There is no specific treatment.

PASTEURELLA MULTOCIDA INFECTION

Not notifiable

Clinical presentation

Lesions usually follow a bite from a dog, cat, human or other animal. The original laceration fails to heal and the skin round it becomes undermined and thin. The ulcer may spread so much that skin grafting may be needed. The same organism may occasionally be found in the sputum of a patient with bronchiectasis.

Investigations

Swabs from the lesions should be taken before antibiotic therapy is commenced and submitted in bacterial transport medium. These will yield growth of *Pasteurella multocida* on blood agar. If injected into a mouse the organism causes septicaemia and typical coccobacilli showing bipolar staining may be seen in blood films.

Incidence

About 300 isolations are made annually in Britain, mainly from animal bites.

Notification

Not needed.

Incubation period

A few days.

Isolation

Not needed.

Period of infectivity

Many animals are probably carriers for an indefinite period; humans soon become noninfective after antibiotic therapy.

Disinfection

Not especially indicated.

School exclusion

Until clinically well.

Contacts

No action needed for ordinary contacts but the biter, human or animal, should be cultured.

Cause and epidemiology

Pasteurella multocida is a small gram negative coccobacillus that may be present in the mouth and gut of many animals.

Prevention

1. Avoid getting bitten; those whose occupation involves the handling of animals that might bite or scratch should wear gloves and other recommended forms of protection.
2. Animal bites should be cleaned immediately.
3. Prophylactic penicillin should be given after animal bites: this is far more useful than the usual ATS.

Treatment

The organism is sensitive to penicillin and this should be given as early as possible; skin grafting may be needed after the infection has subsided.

Clinical presentation

This is an acute virus encephalitis in which the patient first develops headache and pyrexia, a sense of foreboding and paraesthesiae in the vicinity of a recent bite. Muscle spasm, delirium and hydrophobia (spasms brought on by attempts to drink or by merely seeing fluids) are followed by death within a week of the clinical onset.

Investigation

The virus may be detected in mucosal scrapings and skin biopsies by fluorescent antibody staining. It may be isolated by intracerebral mouse inoculation.

Incidence

About one case per year occurs in Britain, always, so far, in persons having been bitten abroad. Although eradicated from this country in 1903 it is still common in Asia and Africa and exists among the wild life in the Americas.

Notification

Statutory, to the M.O.E.H. but informal notification on suspicion would be welcomed.

Incubation period

This depends on the site of the bite and the dosage of infection.

Isolation

There are no modern documented instances of case-to-case infection but the disease is so serious that no risks can be taken, especially as in the terminal stages the virus is widely distributed throughout the patient's body. The patient should be nursed in strict isolation as far as that is compatible with nursing in an intensive care unit; persons attending the patient should have been vaccinated against rabies.

Period of infectivity

Presumably until death and after.

Disinfection

Of saliva and articles contaminated with saliva.

School exclusion

Not likely to apply.

Contacts

See "Isolation". No action is needed for casual contacts.

Cause and epidemiology

The disease is caused by a "bullet-shaped" virus that is a natural disease of animals. In urban areas dogs are important vectors; in rural areas foxes and other wild animals act as a reservoir of infection. Infection in man is nearly always from a dog except perhaps in the U.S.A. where skunks, foxes and bats are commoner sources of infection. Infection is usually through a bite but may rarely occur through a scratch or lick.

Prevention

1. Strict quarantine of all animals imported into this country.
2. *Vaccination*—the recently introduced human diploid cell vaccine is much superior to any previously used.
   a. Vaccination *before* exposure—this should be offered to all who deal with imported animals. Two intramuscular doses of 1·0 ml human diploid cell vaccine are given with an interval of 4 weeks and a reinforcing dose 12 months later.
   b. Vaccination after exposure may prevent the disease developing in patients already infected. In deciding whether or not to vaccinate the following questions must be asked:
      1) Does rabies occur in the country of exposure? It is absent at present from Britain, Australia, New Zealand, Japan, Hawaii, Taiwan, West Indies, Norway and Sweden.
      2) Was the animal kept for examination?
      3) If so, did it become ill and die? Rabid dogs die within a week or so after symptoms commence; there are no healthy carriers.
      4) Was it an animal that had been allowed to roam loose or a well contained pet?
      5) Was a diagnosis of rabies confirmed by a laboratory?
      6) Did the patient come into actual contact with the animal's saliva?

      If after these questions have been answered there is any doubt then vaccination should be carried out; human diploid vaccine has rendered the procedure more efficient, with fewer side effects and less discomfort and with fewer injections.

1·0 ml of vaccine is given intramuscularly on days 0, 3, 7, 14, 30 and 90. At the same time but at a different site an intramuscular injection of antirabies serum is given; with horse antiserum give 20 iu/kg; with human antiserum give 10 iu/kg.

Vaccine for pre-exposure vaccination of persons approved by the D.H.S.S. may be obtained from the Central Public Health Laboratory, Colindale or through the local Public Health Laboratory.

Vaccine for private use may be obtained from Servier Laboratories Ltd, Servier House, Horsenden Lane South, Greenford, Middlesex UB6 7PW, telephone 01-998-2939.

Treatment

One doubtful case of recovery from rabies has been recorded, following tracheostomy, artifical respiration, curarisation and general intensive care.

RESPIRATORY TRACT INFECTION

A. Upper respiratory tract infections
   Bacterial:
   1. b-haemolytic streptococcal tonsillitis.
   2. Diphtheria.
   3. Vincent's angina.

   Viral:
   4. Adenovirus infection.
      Coxsackievirus A infection (p. 16).
      Coxsackievirus B infection (p. 19).
      Infectious mononucleosis (p. 82).
      Primary herpes simplex infection (p. 63).

B. Lower respiratory tract infections
   Bacterial:
      Lobar pneumonia ⎫ These infections are
      Bronchopneumonia ⎬ outside the scope of
      Acute bronchitis ⎭ these notes.
   5. Whooping cough.

   Viral:
   6. Influenza.
   7. Parainfluenza infections.
   8. Respiratory syncytial virus infections.
   9. Psittacosis.*
   10. Q fever.*
   11. *Mycoplasma pneumoniae* pneumonia.*

---

* Although these are not viral infections they behave rather as if they were
and are often dealt with in a virus laboratory.

STREPTOCOCCAL SORE THROAT (Including scarlet fever)
Notifiable as scarlet fever

Clinical presentation
The throat is sore and painful with congested fauces and tonsils specked with exudate. The onset is sudden, the submandibular lymph nodes are enlarged and painful and the tongue has a strawberry-like appearance. The rash, when present, is erythematous with small raised flecks and begins on the face and spreads to the trunk. Peeling is usually slight and occurs about a week after the appearance of the rash.

Investigations
Throat swabs submitted in bacterial transport medium should yield a heavy growth of b-haemolytic streptococci, usually group A.

Incidence
Streptococcal sore throat is common, particularly in children; scarlet fever is less common and less severe than 50 years ago.

Notification
Scarlet fever is still notifiable to the M.O.E.H.; streptococcal sore throat is not.

Incubation period
1 to 3 days.

Isolation
Not usually needed, but if there is a pregnant woman approaching term in the household it might be as well to admit the patient to an isolation block.

Period of infectivity
Up to 24 hours after the commencement of antibiotic therapy.

Disinfection
Of articles soiled by saliva or discharge.

School exclusion
Until clinically recovered and after antibiotic therapy.

Contacts

Normally no action is needed, but when an infection occurs in an institution it is sometimes wise to take throat and nose swabs of contacts so that carriers may be segregated and treated prophylactically.

Cause and epidemiology

95% of cases are caused by group A haemolytic streptococci, the remainder by other groups. The rash in scarlet fever is caused by a toxin and this seems to be identical for different types of group A streptococci because recurrent streptococcal throat infections commonly occur but the rash happens only once to a given patient. Other forms of infection include impetigo, erysipelas and puerperal fever although the last two are rare at present. Non-infectious complications such as nephritis and rheumatic fever are also uncommon today.

Prevention

1. When outbreaks occur in institutions carriers should be segregated and treated prophylactically with penicillin G, 250 to 500 mg every 4 hours, which will soon prevent further excretion.
2. In infectious disease hospitals, *etc.*, children with streptococcal infections should be nursed in individual cubicles to avoid cross infection with types of group A streptococci other than that causing the original infection.
3. Children who have suffered an attack of acute rheumatic fever should be given 500 mg oral penicillin twice daily over an indefinite period, preferably until adolescence.

Treatment

Treatment not only reduces the period of illness but also both reduces the risk of noninfectious complications and rapidly renders the patient noninfectious.

Oral penicillin, 250 to 500 mg every 4 hours for 10 days should be given; if the patient is sensitive to penicillin, erythromycin in a dosage of 250 to 500 mg every 6 hours may be given for 10 days.

DIPHTHERIA *Notifiable*

Clinical presentation

There is usually a grey membrane covering the inflamed fauces in a patient who has not been completely or recently vaccinated against the infection. *The diagnosis must be made on a clinical basis* so that isolation and treatment may commence before laboratory confirmation.

Investigations

Throat and nose swabs (each nostril swabbed separately) should be submitted in bacterial transport medium. *Corynebacterium diphtheriae* will be isolated and tested for toxin production.

Incidence

At present about 6 cases occur in Britain each year.

Notification

Statutory to the M.O.E.H. but he should be notified informally on suspicion.

Incubation period

2 to 5 days.

Isolation

The patient should be kept in an isolation hospital or block until 2 consecutive daily swabs are negative, taken at least 24 hours after stopping antibiotics.

Period of infectivity

Untreated cases—3 or 4 weeks; when antibiotics are used the patient becomes noninfectious within a day or so.

Disinfection

Of articles that have come into close contact with the patient especially those contaminated by nasal or oral discharge.

School exclusion

Patients and contacts—until bacteriologically clear and at the discretion of the M.O.E.H.

Contacts

Nose and throat swabs should be taken from *all* contacts, at home, school and work. Carriers should be isolated and treated with erythromycin, 250 mg 4 times a day for 7 days and retested after the end of treatment. Children who have never been immunised should be given a full course of toxoid and protected with penicillin or erythromycin while immunity is developing; children previously immunised should be given a booster dose of toxoid; adult contacts may be schick tested* and the susceptibles immunised with TAF or alternatively all may be immunised with TAF, risking the possibility of mild reactions.

Cause and epidemiology

C. diphtheriae is always contracted from another human case or carrier and the disease should be thought of when dealing with communities where the immunisation programme has been allowed to lapse or in groups with religious objection to immunisation.

Prevention

By active immunisation with triple vaccine according to the recommended schedule (p. 127). A booster dose should be given at school entry. It is essential to keep a high acceptance rate if the disease is to remain rare in this country.

Treatment

1. Antitoxin—20,000 to 100,000 units intramuscularly (i.v. if severe).
2. Penicillin—250 mg 6 hourly, intramuscularly or by mouth.

* Schick test outfits are available from Wellcome.

VINCENT'S ANGINA *Not notifiable*

Clinical presentation

The disease is characterised by the appearance of shallow ulcers on the buccal mucous membrane, often involving the gums; the ulcers are lined with grey pseudomembrane and have hyperaemic edges. The regional lymph nodes are enlarged and painful and the breath is often foul.

Investigations

Films from the ulcers show many untidy spirochaetes and fusiform bacilli.

Incidence

Common, especially in communities with poor dental hygiene.

Notification

Not needed.

Incubation period

Not known.

Isolation

Not needed.

Period of infectivity

The patient is not infectious.

Disinfection

Not especially indicated.

School exclusion

Until clinically well.

Contacts

No action needed.

Cause and epidemiology

The organisms seen in these lesions are present in small numbers in healthy mouths and Vincent's disease may well follow other conditions, such as virus infection (including glandular fever) and poor dental hygiene, in which normally non-pathogenic organisms have been able to multiply and cause infection.

Prevention

Regular dental inspections and treatment if necessary.

Treatment

Local washing with 3% hydrogen peroxide in an equal volume of warm water.

Penicillin, 250 to 500 mg by mouth every 4 hours for a week.

Metronidazole, 200 mg 3 times a day by mouth for a week.

ADENOVIRUS INFECTION   *Not notifiable*

Clinical presentation

1. Upper respiratory tract infection with enlarged regional lymph nodes and varying degrees of conjunctivitis. About 25% of isolations are from such cases.
2. Mild pneumonia—about 10% of isolations are from these cases.
3. Keratoconjunctivitis only—8% of isolations.
4. Pyrexia of unknown origin—nonspecific general illness—20% of isolations.
5. Gastroenteritis—25% of isolations.
6. Whooping cough syndrome.
7. Adenovirus type II may cause acute haemorrhagic cystitis in children.

Investigations

Faeces, throat swabs and conjunctival swabs (the latter two in virus transport medium) yield adenovirus in tissue culture.

Paired sera taken at an interval of 14 to 21 days show a rise in the group antibody level of adenovirus antigen. Urine should be cultured in cases of haemorrhagic cystitis.

Incidence

Probably a very common cause of minor illnesses which are rarely virologically investigated.

Notification

Not needed.

Incubation period

5 to 9 days.

Isolation

Not needed.

Period of infectivity

While the disease is active.

Disinfection

Not especially indicated.

School exclusion

Until clinically well.

Contacts

No action needed.

Cause and epidemiology

There are at present 31 recognised types of adenovirus which vary slightly from each other in their activities. Types 1, 2, 5 and 6 are endemic in most parts of the world, while 4, 7, 14 and 21 frequently cause outbreaks of respiratory disease. In Britain types 1, 2, 3, 4, 5 and 7 are most commonly found and most eye infections are caused by 3, 4, 7 and 10; most nonspecific pyrexial illnesses are due to 1, 2, 3 and 7. Infection is through droplet spread from carriers or cases; the lower numbered types may be present in the tonsils of about 25% of the population.

Prevention

Vaccines are effective but the size of the problem does not seem to warrant their production and use.

Treatment

No specific treatment is available or often needed.

WHOOPING COUGH (PERTUSSIS) *Notifiable*

Clinical presentation

A catarrhal illness, sometimes with the symptoms of croup, in an infant or young child; the irritating cough gets worse and after a week or 10 days becomes paroxysmal and exhausting and is often accompanied with vomiting. Convulsions and pneumonia are possible complications.

Investigations

A pernasal swab taken at the laboratory or submitted in bacterial transport medium yields *Bordetella pertussis* on culture; if swabs are carefully taken and rapidly cultured the vast majority of cases are bacteriologically positive during the first few days. The white blood count shows an increase to 20,000 to 30,000/mm^3, the majority of the cells being lymphocytes.

Incidence

Varies from year to year and with the vaccination acceptance rates of the population. There is a 3 to 4 year epidemic cycle. In 1977 about 17,000 cases were notified but few of these were bacteriologically proven and it is probable that perhaps 10 times as many cases actually occurred.

Notification

Statutory to the M.O.E.H.

Incubation period

7 to 10 days.

Isolation

Cases should be kept away from young infants.

Period of infectivity

The child is highly infectious during the catarrhal stage but becomes noninfectious after about three weeks, even though the whoop persists.

Disinfection

Not especially indicated.

School exclusion

Until clinically well.

Contacts

Quarantine is of little use; remember the disease is not uncommon in adult contacts.

Cause and epidemiology

Bordetella pertussis (formerly *Haemophilus pertussis*) is acquired by droplet spread from contacts, in half the instances living in the same house. The respiratory mucosa is infected and this causes catarrh and symptoms of croup; later the small bronchioles become blocked with viscid mucus and the paroxysmal cough is an attempt to clear them.

Prevention

Vaccine—if the correct strains of *B. pertussis* are included, pertussis vaccine can be highly protective; if infection does occur in vaccinated children it is generally less severe than in non-vaccinated subjects.

Reactions to vaccine—all vaccines give rise to reactions of some sort and those attributed to pertussis vaccine are alleged to be of a more serious nature than those caused by any other vaccine apart from smallpox vaccine. It is difficult to determine whether this is in fact true as brain damage can occur from causes other than vaccination and in many cases cited the relationship between the illness and the vaccination is very tenuous indeed. In this country the incidence of reaction to whooping cough vaccine is very low. If whooping cough were a mild disease there might be some excuse for not vaccinating but it is often severe and sometimes fatal. There is often an unpleasant illness in older children but complete recovery may be confidently expected; it is in very young infants that fatalities occur and for this reason vaccination should be carried out as early in life as possible.

Contraindications to vaccine—any child who appears healthy at the time and has no family history of fits, epilepsy or convulsions should be vaccinated. In the past conditions suggesting allergic states (eczema, asthma, *etc.*) were taken as contraindication to vaccinate with the result that occasionally children who really needed protection against pertussis were not given it.

If there is evidence of even transient cerebral damage after the first injection the course should be abandoned.

Further procedures:

1. Early vaccination—give one injection of vaccine at the end of each of the first 3 months of life (The D.H.S.S. recommends beginning vaccination at the age of 3 months.)
2. The administration of booster doses of vaccine to older children when a new baby is expected in the household.
3. The use of prophylactic erythromycin (25 mg/kg daily). When an older child in a household containing a young infant contracts the disease he should be treated with this antibiotic to control his infectivity and the baby should be given the antibiotic on a prophylactic basis; as about 50% of infections are acquired within the household, this procedure could halve the incidence of the disease.

Treatment

Although the organism is sensitive to certain antibiotics, the administration of these has little effect on the course of the illness although the patient's infectivity is reduced. Treatment consists of careful nursing; when the mother becomes exhausted it is often best to admit the child to hospital.

INFLUENZA   *Not notifiable*

Clinical presentation

Anything from a mild upper respiratory tract infection to a fulminating pneumonia; occasionally sudden death in shock. Sporadic cases seem to occur only at the beginning or end of an epidemic.

Investigation

Because it is important to recognise influenza outbreaks as early as possible it would be very useful if a proportion of cases of respiratory infection occurring in general practice were investigated microbiologically.

A throat swab, submitted in virus transport medium, should yield growth of the influenza virus in monkey kidney cells and in fertile hens eggs.

Paired sera taken at a 14-day interval will show a rise in specific antibody level.

Incidence

In non-pandemic years about 1000 deaths occur in Britain; although children under 14 years of age are most frequently affected, most deaths occur in the over 65 age group.

Notification

Not necessary for a single case but the M.O.E.H. will wish to hear of outbreaks as soon as possible.

Incubation period

1 to 3 days.

Isolation

Not formally necessary but ambulant mild cases should stay at home for a few days to avoid unnecessary spread of infection.

Period of infectivity

During the active stage of the illness.

Disinfection

Only in the hygienic disposal of tissues, *etc.*

School exclusion

Until clinically well.

Contacts

No action needed.

Cause and epidemiology

Infection is caused by influenza viruses A, B and, less commonly, C. It is always acquired from human cases as far as we know but type A viruses identical with human pathogens have been isolated from animals as well as typically animal strains such as equine and swine influenza viruses. It has been suggested that the radically new serotypes that appear every 10 years or so may have arisen through genetic recombination between human and animal strains in areas, such as the far east, where humans and animals live in close proximity.

Influenza A possesses 2 important antigens, haemagglutinin (H) and neuraminidase (N) and pandemics of infection seem to be associated with the emergence of strains with new types of H or N or both:

Puerto Rico(1943)	H0	N1
F.M. (1947)	H1	N1
Japan (1957)	H2	N2
Hong Kong(1968)	H3	N3
"Red flu" (1978)	H1	N1

Apart from these major changes of antigenicity of H and N, smaller changes occur over shorter periods so that it is important to include in any vaccine strains of virus that are currently causing the disease.

Prevention

Influenza vaccine seems to be only moderately successful in preventing infection but it does seem to reduce the death rate in the old or in those with chronic heart or lung disease. At present both "whole virus" and purified haemagglutinin and neuraminidase are available but attenuated live vaccines are not in current use in this country.

There is evidence that "routine" annual vaccination against influenza is of little value in protecting against infection and may even reduce immunity, so that the following policy is recommended:
1. *Between pandemics* (*i.e.* in years when no radically new antigenic

type of influenza virus is expected)—Vaccinate, every few years (*i.e.* not *every* year) school children over 8 years of age, elderly people in institutions, some key personnel and those suffering from heart, lung or kidney disease or diabetes. Use a vaccine containing the current strains of virus and give 2 doses with a 4 to 6 week interval to age groups who may have missed previous exposure to any of the current strains.
2. *During pandemics* (*i.e.* in years when there is evidence that a strain of virus with a completely new H or N antigen is causing infection in other parts of the world)—Vaccinate everybody with a vaccine containing the new strain; vaccinate early and give 2 doses if there is time.

Treatment

There is no specific treatment. If bacterial superinfection is suspected give antibiotics early.

In severe shock give hydrocortisone (100 to 300 mg intravenously) immediately and continue to give it by saline drip.

PARAINFLUENZA VIRUS INFECTION

Not notifiable

Clinical presentation

Croup in a child of about 4 years of age or bronchiolitis or pneumonia in a younger child. Pharyngitis, laryngitis or tracheitis in adults.

Investigations

The virus may be isolated in monkey kidney cells from throat swabs submitted in virus transport medium. The presence of the virus in the cells is indicated by the fact that when treated with human group O cells the latter stick firmly to the tissue culture cells—a phenomenon known as haemadsorption.

Incidence

All adults will have been infected by types 1, 2 and 3. By the age of 5 up to 100% of children will have been infected by type 3; over 60% of children over 5 will possess antibodies to the other types.

Notification

Not needed.

Incubation period

Probably less than 6 days.

Isolation

From other infants.

Period of infectivity

During the active illness.

Disinfection

Not especially indicated.

School exclusion

Until clinically well, if applicable.

Contacts

No action needed.

Cause and epidemiology

There are 4 recognised human types of parainfluenza viruses; types 1 and 2 cause epidemics at approximately 2 year intervals; type 3 is endemic. Infections with type 1 occur mainly in the winter while those due to type 3 occur all the year round. Infection may occur during the first months of life even in the presence of maternal antibody. At this stage infection is associated with illness but reinfections occur repeatedly and are progressively less accompanied with clinical illness. Adults may occasionally suffer from upper respiratory tract infections, especially pharyngitis. This group of viruses is the second commonest cause of croup in infants after the respiratory syncytial virus.

Prevention

Many attempts have been made to prevent the disease by vaccination but these have failed so far; this may be due to the fact that the virus multiplies in the surface cells of the bronchial mucosa where access by circulating antibodies is difficult. Best results so far have been by the use of attenuated live virus intranasally.

Treatment

There is no specific treatment; antibiotics are not indicated.

RESPIRATORY SYNCYTIAL VIRUS INFECTION

Not notifiable

Clinical presentation

Bronchiolitis or pneumonia in a child under 4 years of age.

Investigation

The virus is very labile and tissue culture tubes should be inoculated at the bedside. Typical syncytia appear in sensitive cells in 3 to 10 days. In older children and adults a rise in the level of complement fixing antibody may be looked for but young infants produce antibody rather poorly.

Incidence

All adults possess antibody; in infants and young children re-infections appear to take place annually, causing progressively less illness as in the case of the parainfluenza viruses.

Notification

Not needed.

Incubation period

4 to 5 days.

Isolation

Any infant with symptoms of croup or bronchiolitis should be isolated from other infants. Cross infection due to this virus is well documented.

Period of infectivity

In young infants, during the active illness; there is evidence that adults can act as healthy or only slightly affected carriers.

Disinfection

Not especially indicated.

School exclusion

Not usually applicable.

Contacts

No action needed.

Cause and epidemiology

The respiratory syncytial virus resembles the parainfluenza viruses in morphology and pathogenicity. It causes bronchiolitis and pneumonia in young infants, reaching a peak incidence at the age of 2 months. Although practically all young babies are infected with this virus, many infections must be subclinical as 1% or fewer are ill enough to require hospital admission. In Britain infection begins to increase each winter with a peak in early March; about 70% of cases are in children under 1 year old; in children between 1 and 4 years of age over 10% have neurological symptoms, particularly convulsions.

Prevention

Killed vaccines have been used but children immunised with these developed severe pneumonia when infected with respiratory syncytial virus—probably an allergic phenomenon (cf. vaccination with killed measles virus). Attenuated live virus vaccines used so far either possessed too much residual pathogenicity or resulted in the patient shedding large amounts of virus that was genetically different from the vaccine strain.

Treatment

There is no specific treatment; antibiotics are not indicated.

PSITTACOSIS (ORNITHOSIS)   *Not notifiable*

Clinical presentation

An unexplained pyrexia with severe sweating, sore throat and cough. There are minimal signs of lung involvement but X-rays suggest a degree of consolidation that is more severe than the patient's condition suggests. Most severe cases appear to be connected with psittacine birds from pet shops or in aviaries. Pigeons, turkeys and other birds may also act as vectors.

Investigations

Paired sera, taken with an interval of 14 days, show a rise in specific complement fixing antibody. Isolation of the causative organism is not usually attempted. For technical reasons it is not possible to carry out complement fixation tests on blood from suspected birds but stained films from spleen cells show typical inclusion bodies. The complement fixation test is also positive in cases of lymphogranuloma venereum, but the clinical pictures are, of course, quite different from each other.

Incidence

About 150 diagnosed cases annually in Britain.

Notification

Although not statutorily notifiable, the M.O.E.H. should be notified of cases, especially when arising in or from a pet shop or commercial aviary.

Incubation period

1 to 3 weeks.

Isolation

Case-to-case infections do occur so that the patient should be nursed in an isolation ward.

Period of infectivity

During the active illness.

Disinfection

Of sputum from patients and of pet shops and aviary premises when these are implicated.

School exclusion

Until clinically well.

Contacts

Colleagues working in pet shops or aviaries implicated should be told to consult their doctor if they develop pyrexia or a cough within 3 weeks of possible exposure.

Cause and epidemiology

The chlamydiae are strictly intracellular organisms that otherwise resemble tiny bacteria. Group A produces lesions of the eye or genitalia, while group B organisms cause ornithosis. The latter is an infection of birds that occasionally spills over into humans. Psittacine birds in particular are frequently healthy carriers that, when well, do not disseminate the organism. With increased stress, as in captivity, a septicaemia develops and the birds suffer from diarrhoea and discharges from the eyes and nostrils so that many organisms are excreted and human infection may follow. Many human cases of ornithosis are subclinical—it may be that strains from psittacine birds are more pathogenic than those from poultry and pigeons. In humans primary infection occurs in the upper respiratory tract followed by septicaemia where the lower respiratory tract is the target organ and a "virus pneumonia" results.

Prevention

Restrictions on the importation of psittacine birds appear to reduce the incidence of severe infections.

Treatment

The organism is very sensitive to chlortetracycline. Give 500 mg 4 times a day for 4 days and then 250 mg 4 times a day for 6 days.

Q FEVER   *Not notifiable*

Clinical presentation

A "virus pneumonia" of abrupt onset with shivering and fever. There are signs of lung involvement and X-rays reveal more extensive consolidation than the patient's condition would suggest. There is practically no mortality but in severe cases convalescence may be prolonged.

Investigations

Paired sera taken with an interval of about 14 days show a rise in the level of specific complement fixing antibody. Isolation of the organism is not routinely attempted.

Incidence

About 100 cases annually in Britain.

Notification

Not statutorily notifiable, but the M.O.E.H. will be glad to be informed of outbreaks.

Incubation period

2 to 4 weeks.

Isolation

Case-to-case infections are rare and the patient may be nursed at home.

Period of infectivity

The patient is not infectious in the normal sense.

Disinfection

Of sputum and articles soiled by sputum.

School exclusion

Until clinically well.

Contacts

No action needed.

Cause and epidemiology

The disease is caused by *Coxiella burneti*, an organism resembling the rickettsiae of typhus but not spread by arthropods nor causing a rash. It commonly infects cattle, sheep and goats. It is moderately resistant to drying, heat and disinfectants and may be conveyed in aerosols, dust and by unpasteurised milk.

Prevention

A vaccine may be prepared but is not worth while considering the small number of cases occurring and the mildness of the disease.

Treatment

Tetracycline, 1 gram immediately followed by 500 mg 4 times a day until the temperature has been normal for 3 days. In the small number of cases that develop Q-fever endocarditis valve replacement under an antibiotic umbrella may be indicated.

MYCOPLASMA PNEUMONIAE INFECTION
(PRIMARY ATYPICAL PNEUMONIA)

Not notifiable

Clinical presentation

Mild pneumonia with pyrexia, unproductive cough, headache and malaise, usually in a child or young adult. X-rays show extensive soft shadows in the lung fields—more extensive than the clinical condition suggests. In addition, 10% of all acute nonbacterial CNS illnesses admitted to hospital in the U.S.A. and Scandinavia are due to *Myco. pneumoniae*.

Investigations

Paired sera taken at an interval of 14 days will show a marked rise in the level of complement fixing antibody to *M. pneumoniae*.

Single sera taken early in the illness may contain cold agglutinins and agglutinins to *Streptococcus* MG. Single sera may also contain specific IgM antibody.

Incidence

One of the commonest causes of mild pneumonia. About 40% of children under 18 possess antibodies which appear protective as second attacks are rare.

Notification

None needed.

Incubation period

9 to 12 days.

Isolation

Not needed.

Period of infectivity

While the disease is active.

Disinfection

Not especially indicated.

School exclusion

Until clinically well.

Contacts

No action needed.

Cause and epidemiology

The disease appeared in military establishments in the U.S.A. in the late 1930s and was named primary atypical pneumonia. The causal organism was for many years believed to be a virus (Eaton's agent) but in 1962 it was found to be a mycoplasma—a small bacterium lacking a cell wall and resembling that causing pleuropneumonia in cattle. There is probably some relationship between mycoplasma infection and the Stevens-Johnson syndrome.

Prevention

No practical methods are available.

Treatment

The organism is sensitive to tetracycline, 1 to 1·5 g daily in divided doses for a week. Kanomycin and erythromycin are also effective.

LEGIONNAIRE'S DISEASE *Not notifiable*
(*LEGIONELLA PNEUMOPHILA* INFECTION)

Clinical presentation

Because they will have been more actively investigated, most cases so far diagnosed have presented with severe pneumonia with patchy consolidation and severe general symptoms, responding poorly to common antibiotics. However, investigation of outbreaks and serological surveys suggest that mild and subclinical infections are not uncommon.

Investigation

Antibody appears fairly early in the disease and may be detected by fluorescent antibody levels. Any antibody level at all in the first few days of illness is suspicious but a single level of 1 in 128 or a 4-fold or greater rise of titre is diagnostic. Most virus laboratories are able to carry out these tests.

Incidence

Probably much commoner than is believed, especially if all minor respiratory infections were completely investigated. Over 1000 cases have been diagnosed as having occurred in the U.S.A. over the last 6 years and more and more are being diagnosed in Britain, including at least one small outbreak.

Notification

Not yet officially notifiable, but the M.O.E.H. should be informed.

Incubation period

Varies with different outbreaks; in the eponymous outbreak in Pennsylvania it was 2 to 10 days; for the "Pontiac fever" it was 36 hours.

Isolation

As we know little about the behaviour of the organism, barrier nursing seems desirable.

Period of infectivity

Not yet known, but probably a few days and even shorter when the appropriate antibiotic has been administered.

Disinfection

Of the sputum only.

School exclusion

Until clinically well.

Contacts

It would seem wise to keep them under surveillance for a few days so that possible respiratory illnesses might be treated as early as possible.

Causes and epidemiology

This illness began as a "mystery disease" following an American Legion convention in Philadelphia in July 1976. About 1·6% of those at risk were attacked and of these 15% died. Very active laboratory investigations showed that the infectious organism was a small gram-negative bacillus that was very difficult to grow. Once it had been cultured it provided material for serological tests. As the organism had never been recognised before it was named *Legionella pneumophila* and 4 serological varieties have so far been described. Examination of sera taken from previous unexplained outbreaks of respiratory infection revealed that several had been caused by this organism, including "Pontiac fever" of 1968, a mild, self-limiting illness with a high attack rate and no deaths. As long ago as 1947 an agent resembling a rickettsia was isolated from a man with upper respiratory infection; this has been shown to be *L. pneumophila*. There is some evidence that the organism may be free-living and possibly disseminated through air-conditioning systems. So far male patients predominate, in a 3:1 ratio.

Prevention

This is not practicable until more is known about the causative organism.

Treatment

Although resistant to many antibiotics, the illness responds to adequate doses of erythromycin. In severe cases large doses should be given (2 to 4 g daily) administered intravenously.

RUBELLA

Clinical presentation

1. Acquired rubella—a mild virus infection with a punctate or fine morbilliform rash, sometimes with slight pyrexia, enlarged post-auricular lymph nodes and sometimes joint pains in adults.
2. Congenital rubella—classically cataracts, heart anomaly and deafness are present; mental retardation may occur and mild degrees of handicap that may not be recognised during the patient's early years.

Investigations

1. Acquired rubella in a non-pregnant patient.

    This may be important if the patient has been in contact with a woman in early pregnancy.

    Paired sera taken at an interval of 14 days will show a rise in the level of haemagglutination inhibiting (HAI) antibody.
2. Acquired rubella in a pregnant woman.

    a. Following a suggestive rash.

    Paired sera taken as above will show a rise in antibody level.

    b. Following contact with a case of rubella.

    If a specimen of serum taken within a few days of contact shows antibody, it may usually be presumed that this antibody was produced in the remote past and the patient is immune.

    c. *But*, if the contact was a child in the woman's household it is just possible that both were infected from a common source about 3 weeks before, so that it is wise in this case to take another specimen 14 days later; if there is a marked rise in antibody, infection has taken place recently.

    d. If a specimen of serum taken immediately after contact is shown to contain no antibody, then the patient is not immune and a further specimen should be taken 21 days later. If this contains no antibody the patient has not become infected but she is not immune and should be vaccinated immediately after delivery.

    If the second specimen shows definite presence of rubella antibody then the woman has experienced a subclinical infection.

3. Diagnosis of congenital rubella.
   a. The cord blood contains an excess of IgM.
   b. This can be shown to be rubella-specific.
   c. The HAI level persists over 6 months (most babies are born with HAI antibodies from the maternal circulation; these disappear over the first 4 to 6 months of life).
   d. The virus may be isolated from the urine and throat in large amounts.
   e. A detectable level of HAI antibody in a child between the ages of 6 months and 4 years is highly suspicious of congenital rubella.
4. Screening of normal women.
   This is carried out using a radial haemolysis (RH) test which gives a roughly quantitative estimate of the amount of antibody present in the serum.

Incidence

Very common, 85 to 90% of adult women have been infected and about 50% of cases are subclinical.

Notification

Acquired rubella is not notifiable in Britain. Congenital rubella, if there are obvious congenital abnormalities, will be reported to the O.P.C.S., usually by the midwife. As many cases of congenital infection may show no abnormality at birth, this method of notification cannot be very efficient.

Incubation period

14 to 21 days.

Isolation

Reverse isolation is needed, pregnant women being kept away from infected cases. Children suffering from rubella are rarely very ill; as they are excluded from school, their mothers will take them shopping or to the hairdresser, to the doctor or the dentist, all situations where contact with a pregnant woman is not unlikely. For this reason it is wise to advise all cases to be kept at home for at least 4 days from the onset of the rash.

Period of infectivity

From about 7 days before to 4 days after the appearance of the rash.

Disinfection

Not especially indicated.

School exclusion

Until 4 days after the onset of the rash.

Contacts

Only those who are pregnant need be investigated.

Cause and epidemiology

The rubella virus is always acquired from another case, overt or subclinical, by droplet infection. The virus multiplies in the upper respiratory tract and then causes a viraemia; the only target organ badly affected is the foetus. When a pregnant woman becomes infected from just before to within the first 3 months of pregnancy the foetus stands a 50 to 80% chance of developing a handicap of some kind.

Cases of congenital infection excrete a large amount of virus over a long period and may be potent sources of infection.

Prevention

It is important that congenital rubella be prevented and this may be done by ensuring that all women of childbearing age are immune. This is done by vaccination—one dose of live vaccine given intramuscularly.
1. Schoolgirls of 11 to 13 years of age are vaccinated at school without prior screening;
2. All other categories are, at present, screened for immunity and only those without antibody are vaccinated; the reason for this is obscure. The following groups should be screened and vaccinated if susceptible:
   a. nurses, teachers and all women coming into contact with children;
   b. all women who will at some time contemplate pregnancy;
   c. all persons, male or female, who constantly come into contact with pregnant women (general practitioners, obstetricians, clinic clerks, medical students, *etc.*).

The only *contraindication* to the vaccination of a susceptible woman is pregnancy. Patients should be instructed not to become pregnant within 2 or 3 months of vaccination. However, if this should accidentally happen the danger seems remote as there are, so far, no reports of handicapped babies being born to women vaccinated in pregnancy who have decided to continue to term. *Normal immuno-*

globulin has not been shown to be of any value in preventing infection; it may be given in large doses in infected women who reject termination.

Treatment

There is no specific treatment either of acquired or congenital rubella.

Clinical presentation

A severe toxaemia caused by the proliferation of *Cl. tetani* at a wound site. There is a gradual development of muscular contraction involving the masseters, abdominal and spinal muscles. In addition to these permanent contractions, muscle spasm occurs with increasing frequency. In mild cases the facial muscles only may be affected but in fatal cases generalised convulsions occur.

The diagnosis is entirely clinical.

Investigations

Swabs from the lesion rarely yield *Cl. tetani* on culture; serological tests are of little use.

Incidence

Usually fewer than 20 cases in Britain each year.

Notification

Statutory, to the M.O.E.H.

Incubation period

4 days to 3 weeks, depending on the location and nature of the wound.

Isolation

Not needed; the patient should be nursed in an intensive care unit.

Period of infectivity

The patient is not infectious.

Disinfection

Not especially indicated.

School exclusion

Until clinically well.

Contacts

No action needed.

Cause and epidemiology

Clostridium tetani is frequently present in the faeces of horses, man and other animals and is consequently frequently found in well manured soil. Injuries of a penetrating nature, especially when there is much dead tissue present, provide an anaerobic environment suitable for growth and toxin production.

Prevention

Vaccine: tetanus toxoid is included in triple vaccine administered in infancy. For a primary vaccination in an adult, 2 doses of 0·5 ml are given with a 6 to 8 week interval followed by a dose of 1·0 ml 6 months later. Too frequent (*e.g.* annual) booster doses do not improve immunity and may cause sensitivity reactions.

Post-exposure prophylaxis: the wound must be opened if necessary, cleaned and dead tissue removed. Further action depends on the patient's vaccination state and the state of the wound.

1. Patient immunised:
   a. Over 5 years ago—0·5 ml tetanus toxoid;*
   b. within last 5 years—no toxoid for clean wounds but 0·5 ml for dirty ones.
2. Patient not immunised:
   a. slight, recent wound—begin primary vaccination;
   b. otherwise, begin primary vaccination and give 1200 mg benzathine penicillin;
   c. wound old and/or badly contaminated—give 250 units human or 1500 units equine antitoxin as above.

Treatment

1. Clean the wound;
2. Administer antibiotics;
3. Give 10,000 units tetanus antitoxin;
4. Nurse with full intensive care facilities.

---

* Plain (*i.e. not* adsorbed) tetanus toxoid should be used for reinforcing doses.

VARICELLA (CHICKENPOX)/HERPES ZOSTER
Not notifiable

Clinical presentation

Chickenpox: the patient is usually a child with a vesicular rash mainly on the non-exposed parts of the body. The vesicles are superficial and appear in successive crops so that there is a marked variation in their sizes. Occasionally the disease is very mild with only a few vesicles. Adults are often severely ill and about 20% develop pneumonia.

Herpes zoster: this is caused by reactivation of the VZ virus that has been lying dormant in the posterior root ganglia. The elderly are most commonly affected but it may occur in children who have suffered a primary chickenpox infection *in utero*. The skin that is supplied by the infected sensory nerves becomes the site of a variable number of vesicles and the cranial nerves may be involved, sometimes causing eye lesions. Unlike the situation with chickenpox, there is often great pain at the site of zoster lesions and this may continue for weeks or months.

Investigation

If laboratory confirmation is required specimens of vesicular fluid should be obtained as suggested under "Herpes simplex infection" (p. 63). The staff of the virus laboratory should be consulted first, as they might wish to obtain the specimen themselves.

Examination is by electron microscopy, when viruses of the herpes type will be seen.

Paired sera will show a rise in complement fixing antibody only in the primary infection (chickenpox) and not after reactivation (herpes zoster).

Incidence

Chickenpox is a very common disease in Britain, 70 to 80% of children under 18 having been infected.

Notification

Not needed.

Incubation period

13 to 17 days.

124

Isolation

At home, until 6 days after the appearance of the rash.

Period of infectivity

Until 6 days after the appearance of vesicles.

Disinfection

Not especially indicated. Domestic washing of bedclothes is adequate.

School exclusion

Until 6 days after the appearance of the last crop of vesicles.

Contacts

No action needed.

Source and epidemiology

The disease is always contracted from other human cases, probably by droplet infection. The virus multiplies in the upper respiratory tract and then invades the bloodstream, spreading to the skin and other target organs, including the lower respiratory tract and the posterior root ganglia; in the latter site the virus hibernates until some "immunological insult" releases it to pass down the sensory nerves and affect the skin supplied by those nerves, causing herpes zoster.

Prevention

1. *In newborn babies*: if a woman develops chickenpox within a week before delivery or during the first weeks of the life of her child, the latter will lack varicella antibody and should be given specific anti-varicella immunoglobulin. This may be obtained from the Central Public Health Laboratory, Colindale, or through the local Public Health Laboratory. The dose is 100 mg contained in 1 ml.
2. *Compromised patients* (p. 130): such patients who become varicella contacts should be given specific hyperimmune immunoglobulin as soon as possible.

Treatment

1. *Varicella*: treatment is needed in severe cases (*e.g.* pneumonia in adults) and in compromised patients. Cytarabine is administered by intravenous transfusion in a dose of 10 to 13 mg/m^2/day.

Acycloguanicine is another drug that shows promise and is being evaluated at present.

2. *Herpes zoster*: this should be treated early with 40% idoxuridine in dimethyl sulphoxide (Herpid) applied constantly to the whole dermatone for 4 days. If the disease is not treated it may cause months of severe pain in older patients.

APPENDIX 1

RECOMMENDED SCHEDULES ON VACCINATION AND IMMUNISATION PROCEDURES

This is a summary of the information given in CMO(78)15 of August 15th, 1978.

First year

Triple vaccine and oral poliomyelitis (1)	At 3 months.
Triple vaccine and oral poliomyelitis (2)	6 to 8 weeks later.
Triple vaccine and oral poliomyelitis (3)	4 to 6 months later.

Second year

Measles vaccine	At least 3 weeks after the last oral poliomyelitis vaccine.

School entry

Triple vaccine and oral poliomyelitis	At least 3 years after completing the basic course.

Between 11 and 13

B.C.G. vaccine	An interval of at least 3 weeks between B.C.G. and rubella.

Between 11 and 13
Girls only

Rubella vaccine

Adults

Poliomyelitis vaccine	A full course for those never immunised. 1. For travellers to an involved country. 2. For unprotected parents of a child to be immunised.

Tetanus	A full course for adults never immunised.

Adult women

Rubella vaccine	For all women of childbearing age who have been found susceptible by screening. Pregnancy must be avoided for at least 2 months after vaccination.

PROPHYLACTIC AND THERAPEUTIC USES OF HUMAN IMMUNOGLOBULINS

Disease and Indications   *Dosage and Source*

Hepatitis type A

Disease and Indications	Dosage and Source
Institutional outbreaks. Travellers to areas with doubtful water supplies. Persons accidentally inoculated with blood negative for HepB surface antigen.	Normal immunoglobulin Under 10 years 250 mg Over 10 years 500 mg Protects 6 to 12 weeks From the local Public Health Laboratory

Hepatitis type B

Inoculation with blood that is HepB surface antigen positive* Newborn babies of mothers who are suffering from type B hepatitis.	From the Central Public Health Laboratory, Colindale. Telephone 01-205-7041 or through the local Public Health Laboratory.

* First ensure that the person inoculated is HepB surface antigen negative.

Measles

A compromised patient† or one suffering from active infection, *e.g.* tuberculosis.	Complete protection: normal immunoglobulin Under 1 year 250 mg 1 to 2 years 500 mg 3 years or over 750 mg
To attenuate the disease.	Normal immunoglobulin; all ages 250 mg From the local Public Health Laboratory.
To reduce vaccine complications in children with a history of epilepsy, chronic heart and lung disease or under developed.	Special low dose immunoglobulin given at time of vaccination and obtained from DCPs

Disease and Indications	*Dosage and Source*

Mumps

Compromised patients† or new-born babies whose mothers develop the disease.

Specific anti-mumps immuno-globulin obtained from Central Public Health Laboratory, Colindale, or through local Public Health Laboratory.

Rubella

There is no evidence that normal immunoglobulin has any protective effect on the foetus of an infected mother.

Tetanus

In patients who have not been actively immunised and where there is a real risk of wound infection (p. 122).

Human immunoglobulin from patients recently boosted from tetanus toxoid.
Available commercially and from sources listed in D.H.S.S. Memorandum HM(70)37 250 units.

Vaccinia

When a compromised patient† *must* be vaccinated.

Specific antivaccinial immuno-globulin obtained from Central Public Health Laboratory or through local Public Health Laboratory.
250 to 1000 mg according to age.

Generalised vaccinia

Full dosage according to age as above repeated in 2 days.

Eye lesions
The use of antiviral drugs such as idoxuridine or trifluoro-thymazine is of more value.

Dosage as above in addition to local instillation of 1% immuno-globulin in sterile saline every 30 minutes.

Varicella/Zoster

Compromised patients†
Babies born of mothers who

Varicella specific immunoglobu-lin.

develop infection around the time of delivery.

Chronically ill children.

Under 1 year	100 mg
1 to 6 years	250 mg
6 to 10 years	500 mg
11 to 14 years	750 mg
15 years and over	1000 mg

Normal immunoglobulin may be used if specific antivaccinial immunoglobulin is not available. This, with the appropriate dosage, may be obtained from the local Public Health Laboratory.

† Compromised patients are those on steroids, cytotoxic drugs or any therapy likely to damage immunity or suffering from hypogamma-globulinaemia, leukaemia, Hodgkin's disease, *etc.*

APPENDIX 3

USE OF THE MICROBIOLOGY LABORATORY

1. *Do not send to the laboratory, at least without making previous arrangments, any patient believed to be suffering from a dangerous or highly infectious disease, e.g.* diphtheria or rubella, because of the danger of infecting other patients, particularly pregnant women.
2. If there is the least suspicion that the patient is suffering from *Lassa fever, Ebola fever, Marburg disease or smallpox contact the M.O.E.H. before taking specimens* (p. 00).
3. *Jaundiced patients*: label both specimen container and application form "High Risk", make sure that the container is leakproof, seal it in a plastic bag and submit the application form separately.
4. Give all the details required and on the correct form; use of the wrong forms causes terrible difficulties in filing and reporting and wastes a lot of laboratory time.
5. *Viral and bacterial transport media* are available from the laboratory; they both have a finite shelf life so that small stocks only should be kept in the surgery; they need not be kept in a refrigerator.
6. *Specimens of faeces*:
   a. These may be obtained by the patient if he covers the water in the W.C. with plenty of toilet paper and then defaecates; he can then rescue a portion of faeces about the size of his thumb and then, using the spoon provided, place it in a widemouthed container without soiling the rim. What is not required may be easily flushed away.
   b. When small babies are being investigated faeces may be scraped from a dirty nappy, *but please ensure that sufficient is provided*.
   c. Specimens of faeces, in clean containers, should be submitted on 3 successive days.
7. *Blood for serology*:
   a. This should be taken into a sterile leakproof container clearly labelled with the patient's name and sent to the laboratory as soon as possible; if there is any delay allow to clot at room temperature. Do not refrigerate.
   b. If the patient has an unexplained temperature, take a specimen of blood and send it to the laboratory; if a firm diagnosis has not been reached a fortnight later, take a second specimen and the laboratory will examine the pair in

parallel, looking for a rise in antibody.

c. *Single specimens* of serum are not generally of great use, but if investigations have been delayed for weeks after the onset of the illness, they may provide limited information and such specimens should be labelled: "Please treat as a single specimen".

8. When *vesicle fluid* is to be examined it may be convenient to send the patient to the laboratory (provided arrangements have been made) or, if this is not possible, for the microbiologist to visit the patient in order to take the specimen.

9. When smears of exudate, *etc.* are required contact the laboratory director as smears may be preferred on special etched slides provided by the laboratory; several slides should be made.

10. *Whooping cough* is best investigated using pernasal swabs; in some cases it may be possible to make an appointment for the swab to be taken by the microbiologist at the laboratory, in others the swabs will be supplied with bacterial transport medium.

11. Some laboratories are interested in providing a rapid diagnostic service, using a fluorescent antibody test, for influenza, measles, parainfluenza, respiratory syncytial virus, herpes, varicella and other infectious agents. If this service is required, arrangements should be discussed with the director of the laboratory.

APPENDIX 4

COMMUNICABLE DISEASE AND OVERSEAS TRAVEL

Advice on the protective procedures recommended for travellers is given in the D.H.S.S. publications: "Immunisation against Infectious Diseases" and "Notice to Travellers". Much of the following is extracted from these.

1. *Official International Certificates**
   These are needed for the purpose of entering certain countries; they are not for the benefit of the holder but for the purpose of protecting the country to be visited from yellow fever and smallpox.
   a. *Yellow fever*
      Countries where the ecology is thought to favour the spread of this disease demand a certificate of vaccination from visitors coming from or passing through certain areas of Africa and South America. The vaccination is, in any case, recommended for the protection of travellers to the latter regions. Vaccination is carried out at the local Yellow Fever Vaccination Centre, the address of which may be obtained from the District Health Office. The vaccination is usually charged for and an appointment has to be made.
   b. *Smallpox*
      Although the last case of smallpox outside the U.K. occurred in October 1977 some countries still demand a valid certificate of vaccination against smallpox and where this is the case the regulations must be complied with; however, when vaccination is merely recommended, this, in the continued absence of the disease, should be resisted. If there is a medical reason why the patient should not be vaccinated a certificate giving that reason should be supplied and stamped and countersigned at the Local Authority office. Vaccine lymph and international certificate forms are obtainable from the District Health Office; after vaccination the completed certificate should be stamped and signed at the Local Authority Office.
   c. *Cholera*
      There is no longer an international certificate for cholera vaccination.
      Vaccination against cholera should best be restricted to

* Note: up-to-date information on overseas vaccination requirements may be obtained from a 24–hour service from Heathrow Airport. Telephone number p. xi.

field workers and others likely to be existing in very unhygienic conditions. Revaccination is needed at 6 month intervals.

Useful inoculations

a. *Typhoid vaccine* (p. 11). This is probably the most useful vaccine for travellers outside northern Europe and North America. A course or booster dose should be given as indicated.
b. *Poliomyelitis vaccine* (p. 14).
   This should be administered to travellers to any underdeveloped country or any country where poliomyelitis is known to occur. A course or booster dose should be given as indicated.

Antimalarial Precautions

These should be initiated at the beginning of the journey if the destination is known to harbour malaria or if there is any possibility of passing through a malarial country *en route*. The appropriate drugs may be obtained from a pharmaceutical chemist but not at Health Service expense and should be continued with for at least 14 days after return (p. 67).

Hepatitis type A

Travellers may be protected against this disease by normal human immunoglobulin (500 to 750 mg). Protection lasts only 6 to 12 weeks so that the inoculation should be given as shortly before departure as possible. It is advisable for all who stay in areas where the water supply may be contaminated, *e.g.* parts of India, and is especially advised for hitch hikers. The immunoglobulin is at present obtainable for this purpose from the local Public Health Laboratory.

Rabies

Rabies vaccination is needed only by those likely to deal with susceptible animals, *e.g.* veterinary surgeons or naturalists. If a traveller is bitten by a dog in a country where rabies occurs he should (1) see the local doctor at once; (2) seek information about the dog—was it vaccinated against rabies? (3) exchange names and addresses with the dog's owner; (4) try to ensure that the dog is quarantined and investigated (p. 89).

APPENDIX 5

COMMUNICABLE DISEASE AND THE SCHOOL

These notes are taken from the Essex Area Health Authority's "Advice to the Education Authority on Communicable Diseases".

1. When advice is required communicate with the Specialist in Community Medicine (Child Health), the School Medical Officer or the M.O.E.H., whoever is the most readily available.
2. Only the head teacher can exclude a child from school but he will be expected to act on the advice of the School Medical Officer (and presumably on that of the child's family doctor).
3. The periods of exclusion given in the tables are the minimum and in many cases it will take longer for the child to become fit for school again.
4. In some instances the contacts of patients should also be excluded (Table 2)
5. Family doctors carry some responsibility to schools for patients suffering from communicable diseases who happen to be members of the school staff.
   a. Teachers who have recovered from pulmonary tuberculosis are required to provide a certificate to the effect that they are no longer infectious (at intervals of 3 months for the first year and 6 monthly for as long as the chest physician considers necessary. These certificates will presumably be provided by the chest physician.
   b. Members of the school staff who contract a communicable disease must be excluded from school in the same way as a child suffering from the same illness.
   c. All female school staff of childbearing age should be advised to undergo screening for rubella and to be vaccinated if shown to be susceptible in view of the specific danger of the school environment in this respect.
   d. Consideration should be given to the advisability of exclusion from work of school meals staff members suffering from septic lesions that might be considered to be a possible source of infection or until bacteriologically cleared after a diarrhoeal infection.

TABLE 1

RECOMMENDED PERIODS OF EXCLUSION FROM SCHOOL

Disease	*Period of Exclusion*
Bacillary dysentery	Until declared fit by the M.O.E.H.
Chickenpox	6 days from the onset of the rash
Diphtheria	Until bacteriologically clear and after discussion with the M.O.E.H.
Food poisoning (including salmonellosis)	Until declared fit by the M.O.E.H.
Rubella	4 days from the onset of the rash
Hepatitis type A	7 days from the onset of jaundice
Impetigo	Until the scabs have disappeared
Measles	7 days from the onset of the rash
Acute meningitis	Until bacteriologically clear and after discussion with the M.O.E.H.
Mumps	Until the swelling has subsided
Pediculosis	Until adequately treated
Poliomyelitis	Until well and after discussion with the M.O.E.H.
Pulmonary tuberculosis	Until declared no longer infectious
Pertussis	21 days after the onset of the paroxysmal cough
Ringworm of the body or scalp	Until adequately treated
Scabies	Until the child and the whole family have been treated
Typhoid fever	At the discretion of the M.O.E.H.

Note

These are the recommendations made by the Essex Area Health Authority to the Education Authority. As they are for the benefit of Head Teachers rather than doctors, they are rather less permissive than those in the text.

TABLE 2

DISEASES IN WHICH CONTACTS SHOULD BE
EXCLUDED FROM SCHOOL

Disease	*Period of Exclusion*
Diphtheria	Until bacteriologically clear and after discussion with the M.O.E.H.
Acute meningitis	After consulting the M.O.E.H.
Poliomyelitis	Home contacts only—at the discretion of the M.O.E.H.
Enteric fever	Home contacts only—at the discretion of the M.O.E.H.

INDEX

in congenital herpes simplex
infection, 63
in malaria, 66
in Weil's disease, 61
"High risk" labels in, 132
Joint pains in rubella, 118

Koplik's spots, 69

Lassa fever, 27, 132
Legionella pneumophila, 116
Legionnaire's disease, 116
Leptospira canicola, 78
Leptospira icterohaemorrhagiae, 62
Listeria monocytogenes, 78
Lobar pneumonia, 77
Lymphocytic meningitis
coxsackievirus type A, 16
coxsackievirus type B, 19
echovirus, 21
herpesvirus, 63
mumps, 84
Lymphogranuloma venereum, 110
Lymphocytosis in whooping cough,
100
Lymphoma, Burkitt's, 83

Malaria, 66
Malarial precautions, 67, 135
Marburg disease, 30, 132
Mastitis in mumps, 84
Maternal antibody
in cytomegalovirus infection, 8
in parainfluenza, 107
in respiratory syncytial infection,
108
in rubella, 118
in varicella, 125
Maternal infections
hepatitis type B, 60
cytomegalovirus infection, 8
rubella, 120
varicella, 125
Meningitis, 71
amoebic, 78
coxsackievirus A, 16
coxsackievirus B, 19
echovirus, 21
herpes simplex, 63
leptospiral, 78
listerial, 78
mumps, 84

meningococcal, 72
pneumococcal, 76
tuberculous, 78
Measles, 69
Mental retardation
cytomegalovirus infection, 7
rubella, 118
Membrane
in diphtheria, 94
in Vincent's angina, 96

Naegleria fowleri, 78
Needles, hypodermic, 59
Neisseria meningitidis, 72
Nephritis, post streptococcal, 93
Neuraminidase, influenzal, 104
Norwalk virus, 53

Ocular lesions
herpetic, 63
vaccinial, 130
Oophoritis, in mumps, 84
Orchitis, in mumps, 84
Ornithosis, 110
Overseas vaccination requirements
service telephone number, xi

Pancreatitis, in mumps, 84
Paraesthesiae, in rabies, 88
Parainfluenza infection, 106
Paralysis
in poliomyelitis, 13
in coxsackie A infection, 16
in coxsackie B infection, 19
in echovirus infection, 21
Paratyphoid fevers, 10
Parvovirus gastroenteritis, 52
Pasteurella multocida, 86
Paul–Bunnell reaction, 83
Pediculosis, 137
Pericarditis, Coxsackie B, 19
Pernasal swab in whooping cough,
100, 133
Pharyngitis
in coxsackie A infections, 16
in parainfluenza virus infections,
106
Pigeons, 110
Picornaviruses, 12
Plasmodium falciparum, 67
Plasmodium malariae, 67
Plasmodium ovale, 67